Lifted

A Christian's Guide to Ditching Depression and Discovering Joy

Lauren Rice

Bill Rice
RANCH

Lifted

Scripture quotations are taken from the *Holy Bible*, King James Version.

Printed in the United States of America.

I will extol thee, O LORD; for thou hast **lifted** me up.
—Psalm 30:1

CONTENTS

Part 1:
Diagnosing the Problem

Chapter One

Addressing the Elephant in the Room

Once upon a time, a pig-tailed little girl lived in a good and happy family. She spent her summers chasing butterflies by day and fireflies by night, eating watermelon, and making new friends. She saw good in everyone she met and liked almost everyone she met, too. Animals were not an exception to that rule. She took in stray dogs when her parents would let her and even tried to nurse a few sick baby birds back to health. Like most little girls, she didn't like school too much but loved recess when she could swing her heart out and build castles in the sky. Most people would have described this little girl as a dreamer and an optimist.

But life happens. And life happened to this happy little girl. As she grew up, she began to face new challenges, as all young women do. Her senior year of high school, the family decided to move two states away from home. She had to leave her friends and church family and start from scratch at a completely new church and school. Making new friends in high school wasn't as easy as it had been in elementary school. It wasn't long after the move before her best friend from back home slowly faded off the scene. The texts and phone calls were less and less frequent until finally it was as if her friend had fallen off the face of the earth. She had been forgotten. A workout injury that caused her to be cut from the school volleyball team didn't help matters either. By the end of her senior year, she found out that she did not get accepted into her dream college. Her dreams seemingly dashed, she decided to apply at another school and study accounting, as her parents had suggested.

College, with all its firsts, drama, and dorm life, excited her. That is, until her boyfriend broke up with her over another girl. Just when things looked bleak enough, she heard the dreaded words from her mother—her dad had cancer. Before she knew it, everything that had come so easily for her as a child—things like faith, hope, and joy—were slipping through her fingers. She didn't have the strength to try to grip them any longer. She let them go.

Each morning, when she opened her eyes, a feeling of disappointment washed over her, as if she had hoped that she wouldn't wake up. Every day seemed like an uphill trek, with every little ordinary task exhausting her. The more she dwelt on her perceived failures, appearance, and inabilities, the more she disliked herself. She wished she could be someone different. Soon, this became her default thought process.

Daily tasks like getting out of bed and getting ready for work became exhausting. The hobbies and interests that used to inspire and cheer her now felt dull and pointless. She couldn't focus when she tried to read. When friends invited her to parties and social events, she found an excuse not to go. Leaving the house just wasn't worth the stomach cramps and fatigue. To her dismay, she found herself snapping at her loved ones because any little thing could irritate her. Sometimes, she would cave to intense food cravings and then lie on the couch to recover from the binge. Other times, eating was too unappetizing to think about! Anxiety attacks and crying would flare up without warning, nearly every day. Sleep, when it did come, was a welcome guest because it offered a reprieve from the dark feelings of hopelessness and worthlessness. She talked about her dreams and plans when people asked, but on the inside, she felt apathetic toward them. Over time, she had swallowed the lie that she had nothing to offer the world and that the world had nothing to offer her.

We might call this girl's experience a struggle with depression. If you've picked up this book, chances are that you can relate to this girl on some level. The circumstances surrounding your struggle may be much worse, or perhaps there are seemingly no extenuating circumstances. Questions like, "Why do I feel this way?" or "When will this ever end?" may be swirling around in your mind.

Before we can diagnose the problem, we must first address the elephant in the room! While this type of mental anguish may be common, it is also one of the most difficult issues to talk about. As C.S. Lewis put it, "Mental pain is less dramatic than physical pain, but it is more common and also more hard to bear. The frequent attempt to conceal mental pain increases the burden: it is easier to say, 'My tooth is aching' than to say, 'My heart is broken.'"[1] While less visible than physical pain, mental pain can be just as devastating.

We must define the faceless fiend we call depression. According to *Medical News Today*, "Depression is a mood disorder that involves a persistent feeling of sadness and loss of interest. It

1 C. S. Lewis, *The Problem of Pain*, (New York, NY: Harper One, 1940), 161.

is different from the mood fluctuations that people regularly experience as part of life."[2] Depression is a prolonged period of feelings of sadness, worthlessness, and hopelessness. Medical News Today goes on to explain that "Depression is an ongoing problem, not a passing one. It consists of episodes during which symptoms last for at least 2 weeks."[3] The Anxiety and Depression Association of America says, "Major depression is characterized by having at least five of the nine common symptoms."[4] Those symptoms might include overwhelming feelings of sadness or a loss of interest and pleasure in most usual activities, decrease or increase in appetite, insomnia or hypersomnia, excessive or inappropriate guilt, recurrent thoughts of death and suicidal ideation with or without specific plans for committing suicide, and cognitive difficulties, such as a diminished ability to think, concentrate, and make decisions.[5] As this list of symptoms indicates, there are many levels and types of depression. Some who experience it may despair of life, while others may simply wish to escape their problems.

Depression is like a storm cloud that lingers with its victims for years, and downpours on them in intervals. The storm doesn't give a warning—it just comes when it wants to. Circumstances, hormonal imbalances, and even genetics can trigger depression in different people. Certain personalities may be more susceptible to depression than others. Since both external circumstances and internal circumstances can contribute to depression, it does not look the same for every person who struggles with it. The grooves that depression makes in our minds go deep, so we can't

---

2 Laura Goldman, "What is depression and what can I do about it?," *Medical News Today*, last medically reviewed by Nicole Washington on August 5, 2022, https://www.medicalnewstoday.com/articles/8933.

3 Ibid.

4 "What is depression?," Anxiety and Depression Association of America, last updated January 18, 2023, https://adaa.org/understanding-anxiety/depression.

5 Ibid.

expect to get over it in one day. We shouldn't be discouraged if the process takes months or even years. Just as the downward spiral was gradual, so undoing the damage of depression is gradual.

How is a Christian supposed to deal with depression? Whatever the cause, the answer to end this harmful cycle is *not to deny* that we have these thoughts or feelings, but to look outside ourselves for the answer. While the symptoms and circumstances of depression vary for different people, we were all created by the same loving God, and He can help us to ditch depression.

Chapter Two

Kicking Complexes

Perhaps you can relate to the symptoms we've just discussed. What now? Often Christians face two unique roadblocks to diagnosing and getting help with depression. Next, let's look at how we can nudge the elephant out of the room by removing these roadblocks to recovery!

The Good Christian Complex

The first roadblock is what we will call the good Christian complex. A Christian struggling with depression may feel even more isolated than a non-Christian. You know that Christians should be the most joyful people on the planet. Christians are to be characterized by the joy of the Lord, and when you are not, the doubt about your status as a good Christian only deepens the pain.

When you look around and see the joy of other Christians, you think that you must not tell anyone about your problem. You assume that if you do, they will deem you not really a Christian or, at least, not a good Christian. You may even begin to doubt your own salvation! If a good Christian is supposed to be characterized by the joy of the Lord, and you aren't, then that must mean you aren't really a Christian! Before long, you are trapped between protecting your image as a good Christian and doubting your own status as a Christian in the first place.

Assurance of Salvation

When depression causes us to doubt our own salvation, we must look to something that does not fluctuate with our feelings.
I John 5:11 says that God's Word is the record which tells us whether we are saved. What does the record of God's Word say? It says in I John 5:12, *"He that hath the Son hath life."* If you have made the conscious choice to trust Jesus Christ to forgive your sins and give you a home in heaven, then you have the Son and the life that only He provides. If you have accepted Jesus alone as your Savior, then God has also accepted you as His child. John 1:12 puts it this way: *"But as many as received him* [that's Jesus], *to them gave he power to become the sons of God, even to them that believe on his* [Jesus'] *name."* The words receive and believe mean essentially the same thing. When we receive or accept Jesus as our only way to heaven and believe or depend on Him to get us there, we are accepted into God's family. We are saved! We must judge our status by God's Word, not our battle with depression.

Eternal Security

When we are saved and given that life I John 5 speaks about, it is not a short-lived or reversible transaction. Returning to I John 5:11, we see that *"God hath given to us eternal life."* If it is eternal, then it never ends. Since nothing we felt or did got us saved in the first place, nothing we feel or do can get us unsaved! The words of our Lord Jesus Christ put the good Christian complex to rest. In John 10:28-29, Jesus told His disciples, *"And I give unto them eternal life; and they shall never perish, neither shall any man pluck them out of my hand. My Father, which gave them me, is greater than all; and no man is able to pluck them out of my Father's hand."* There it is again: the life that God gives is eternal, never-ending, real life!

Our feelings are no match for God's Word. Feelings change; God's Word does not. God's Word says that every child of God is kept in Jesus' hand, and not in His only, but also in the Father's hand. We are doubly held by our Savior! God promises that nothing we could ever think, feel, or do will ever change our status as His child. The same God who got us saved is the only One who keeps us saved. We can never lose our salvation because the Father holds us securely in His hand forever. Depression doesn't change that fact. Our feelings that tell us otherwise are not from God. They are from our enemy the devil.

Our enemy the devil rarely tells us a boldfaced lie. Rather, he begins by planting seeds of doubt in our minds. Like he did to Eve in the garden, he will whisper to us, "Hath God said?" The moment we hear that question, we must fight back with, "God hath said." We must remind ourselves of Christ's promise in John 10:28-29. The devil wants us to doubt, but the One who is greater than he greater than all holds us in the palm of His hand.

So, banish from your mind the thought that just because you are battling depression you must not be a Christian or at least not a good Christian. As we will see in the next roadblock, even *good* Christians can battle depression.

The Lone Ranger Complex

Another roadblock is the lone ranger complex. This is the idea that you are the only one who understands what you are going through. It is also the idea that asking for help is weakness. You think that you must suffer in silence and muster the strength to help yourself.

This way of thinking is understandable. Sometimes, all you can see are the smiles of other Christians on Sunday morning. Everyone looks so happy, and it only makes you feel more alone in your depression. This complex may lead you to believe that no other Christian has struggled with depression like you have. Especially if you have struggled with suicidal thoughts or ideations, you may assume that no other Christian you know could possibly understand your experience. The doubt, now compounded with isolation, drives you further into your depression. You are afraid you cannot be open with anyone else about your struggle because they would only judge you for having such a problem. You assume that you must be strong and go through it alone because no one else would understand.

The fact is that more people may understand than you assume. Just as you may be able to paste on a smile on Sunday morning, others can do so just as well. There is always more brewing beneath the surface than you could know unless you ask. This is not to say that every smiling Christian at your church on Sunday morning is depressed. However, more of them may be able to comprehend your problem and show compassion than you think.

Depression and the Christian Experience

Depression is not any more foreign to the Christian experience than anger or cancer is to the Christian experience. For example, a 2014 study of Acute Mental Illness and Christian Faith, conducted by Lifeway Research, found that within the Protestant denominations, "74% of pastors personally knew one or more people who had been diagnosed with clinical depression."[1] More Christians struggle with this today than we think. And they always have. One famous and mightily used preacher of the nineteenth century described such a struggle in his writings. This preacher, C. H. Spurgeon, wrote in his commentary on Psalm 88:

> Some of us can enter into this experience for many a time have we traversed this valley of death shade, and dwelt in it by the month together. Really to die and to be with Christ will be a gala day's enjoyment compared with our misery when worse than physical death has cast its dreadful shadow over us. Death would be welcome as a relief by those whose depressed spirits make their existence a living death. Are good men ever permitted to suffer thus? Indeed, they are.[2]

Spurgeon, the prince of preachers, understood the experience that we call depression. He knew it intimately. Perhaps you haven't felt it as severely as Spurgeon describes here, but

---

1 Jennifer Huang Harris, MD, Harold G. Koenig, MD, and John R. Peteet, MD, "Downcast: Do Real Christians Get Depressed?," Christian Medical & Dental Associations, May 7, 2020, https://cmda.org/downcast-do-real-christians-get-depressed/#_edn1.

2 C. H. Spurgeon, "Psalm 88 by C. H. Spurgeon," Blue Letter Bible, last modified December 5, 2016, https://www.blueletterbible.org/Comm/spurgeon_charles/tod/ps088.cfm.

whatever the degree, your experience is not unusual to good Christians.

Some of the those good Christians that have been permitted to suffer through depression are people we might call our favorite Bible characters. Just because we learned about their highlight reels in Sunday School doesn't mean they weren't real people with real problems. Let's consider some mightily used but very human Bible characters who suffered through depression.

Job

Because of his horrible circumstances, Job despaired of life. In Job 3:11, he cries, *"Why died I not from the womb? Why did I not give up the ghost when I came out of the belly?"* The emotional, spiritual, mental, and physical pain that Job felt after all the tragedies in his life made Job wish that he had never been born. If he simply did not exist, he would never have to suffer like this. Job's story demonstrates that sometimes depression can simply be a reaction to the circumstances of life. Traumatic life events can trigger depression, like it did for Job.

Elijah

Exhausted, lonely, and discouraged, Elijah felt his ministry and his life were worthless. I Kings 19:4 says, *"But he himself went a day's journey into the wilderness, and came and sat down under a juniper tree: and he requested for himself that he might die; and said, It is enough; now, O LORD, take away my life; for I am not better than my fathers."* We remember Elijah as the great man of God who stood before kings, performed miracles, and ushered revival into his nation. Yet we find Elijah in a very dark place here. In this moment, Elijah had obeyed God only to find himself hunted like an animal, running, hiding, and alone.

Being alone was the kicker for Elijah. He thought that he was the only one left serving God. From Elijah's story, we can see that sometimes sheer exhaustion and discouragement can plummet us into depression.

Jonah

Perhaps not usually thought of as a stellar example, Jonah was nevertheless a prophet greatly used of God. Jonah experienced a low in his life right after a high. He had just been rescued from the belly of a whale and given a second chance, when he was hit with another reality that did not align with his plans. Jonah became so disappointed in God's plan and so angry with God that he wanted God to kill him. He moans in Jonah 4:3, *"Therefore now, O LORD, take, I beseech thee, my life from me; for it is better for me to die than to live."* Jonah's life teaches us that sometimes depression is a result of disappointment in and anger at God for the way things have turned out in our lives.

David

The sweet psalmist, David, was also the author of many melancholy songs. Certainly, David was acquainted with trouble in his life. He had experienced disappointment, betrayal, abandonment, and doubt in God's plan. Here are just a few of his psalms, describing such times in his life:

Psalm 6:3, 6-7 says, *"My soul is also sore vexed . . . I am weary with my groaning; all the night make I my bed to swim; I water my couch with my tears. Mine eye is consumed because of grief."* Have you ever felt such extreme sadness that you cried all night? David did too.

In Psalm 13:1-2, David cries, *"How long wilt thou forget me, O LORD? For ever? How long wilt thou hide thy face from me? How long shall I take counsel in my soul, having sorrow in my heart daily?"* Have you ever felt like sorrow is a daily experience for you? Have you ever wondered how long this feeling would last? So did David.

Psalm 55:2, 4-8 says, *"I mourn in my complaint, and make a noise . . . My heart is sore pained within me: and the terrors of death are fallen upon me. Fearfulness and trembling are come upon me, and horror hath overwhelmed me. And I said, Oh that I had wings like a dove! For then would I fly away, and be at rest. Lo, then would I wander far off, and remain in the wilderness. Selah. I would hasten my escape from the windy storm and tempest."* Have you ever wished you could just be a bird so that you could fly away from your problem? Have you ever felt trapped in depression, wishing that you had wings to escape? David can relate.

He exclaims in Psalm 69:1-3, *"Save me, O God; for the waters are come in unto my soul. I sink in deep mire, where there is no standing: I am come into deep waters, where the floods overflow me. I am weary of my crying: my throat is dried."* Have you ever cried until you simply couldn't cry anymore? David used up all his tears, too.

David also dealt with times of great anxiety, to the point that his decisions were dictated by fear rather than clear thinking. One such occasion is found in I Samuel 21. In flight from King Saul, David decided to hide himself in the land of the Philistines. When word of David's presence began to spread, David feared that they would remember him as the one who had killed their hero, Goliath. He assumed he would no longer be safe there if they knew who he was. So, David made a choice that, from the outside looking in, seems irrational. But to an anxious person, it makes sense. I Samuel 21:12-13 says, *"And David laid up these words in his heart, and was sore afraid of Achish the king of Gath. And he changed his behavior before them, and feigned himself mad in their hands, and scrabbled on the doors of the gate, and let his spittle fall down upon his beard."* David changed his behavior because of fear. He wanted them to think he was crazy so that they would throw him out of their kingdom rather than keep him and possibly kill him. Has anxiety ever twisted and distorted your character so that you act out of character like David did here?

This wasn't the only time during his season of running from Saul that David allowed anxiety to dictate his decisions. In fact, David went back to Gath, the land of the Philistines and King Achish! I Samuel 27:1 gives David's reasoning: *"And David said in his heart, I shall now perish one day by the hand of Saul: there is nothing better for me than that I should speedily escape into the land of the Philistines; and Saul shall despair of me, to seek me any more in any coast of Israel: so shall I escape out of his hand."* Anxiety caused David to think in either-or terms. David believed that either he would hide among the Philistines or Saul would surely kill him! Now, it is easy for you and me to see that David was irrational here because David had God's promise that he would be the next king. God would not allow Saul to kill David because David had to live to be the next king. Yet anxiety blinded David to God's promises so that all he could see was the danger of the moment. He went into fight or flight mode. David gave in to hopelessness, and as a result, he felt that his only option was to run back to Achish, the enemy king.

We can be this way, too. We have God's promises of unfailing love (Romans 8), of His constant presence with us (Hebrews 13:5), of His good plan for us (Jeremiah 29:11). Yet we may give in to the desperation and hopelessness that anxiety and depression breed, believing that we have no other choice but to. . . fill in the blank. Some have thought they had no other choice but to run and hide. Others have allowed anxiety and depression to convince them that they had no other choice but to take their own lives. These are lies that do not have to dictate your decisions. You have promises from God, just as David did. Fight back the lies with God's Word.

From these examples of David's writing, we see that seasons of prolonged stress, fear, or grief can spiral into anxiety and depression. Anxiety and depression can then warp our reasoning so that we can no longer make wise choices.

Asaph

Another psalmist, Asaph, was also well acquainted with the depression that stemmed from prolonged seasons of stress, fear, and grief. He described moments of inconsolable sadness. Psalm 77:2-3 says, *"In the day of my trouble I sought the Lord: my sore ran in the night, and ceased not: my soul refused to be comforted. I remembered God, and was troubled: I complained, and my spirit was overwhelmed."* Have you ever been so consumed with sadness that even thinking about God troubled you? Asaph would understand.

Heman

Another psalmist called Heman describes being so smothered with troubles that he felt no better than a dead man. In Psalm 88:3-6,14-15, he exclaimed, *"For my soul is full of troubles: and my life draweth nigh unto the grave. I am counted with them that go down into the pit: I am as a man that hath no strength: free among the dead, like the slain that lie in the grave, whom thou remeberest no more: And they are cut off from thy hand. Thou hast laid me in the lowest pit, in darkness, in the deeps. . . LORD, why castest thou off my soul? Why hidest thou thy face from me? I am afflicted and ready to die."* Spurgeon described Heman as "a man of deep experience, who had done business on the great waters of soul trouble."[3] Have you ever done business on the great waters of soul trouble? Have you ever felt as if you were no better off than a dead man? Have you, like the psalmist, felt that God has lowered you into the deepest darkness? Then you can relate to Heman, the psalmist.

The Afflicted Psalmist

Psalm 102 is simply subtitled, *"A Prayer of the afflicted, when he is overwhelmed, and poureth out his complaint before the LORD."* We don't know this psalmist's name, but we do know that he was afflicted and overwhelmed. Psalm 102:4, *"My heart is smitten, and withered like grass; so that I forget to eat my bread. By reason of the voice of my groaning my bones cleave to my skin."* In this psalm, the oppression of the enemy was so heavy on the psalmist that he forgot to do normal every-day activities. Life, as he had known it, just couldn't continue. Have you ever been so overwhelmed that life just seemed to stop?

Facts and Feelings

These Bible characters demonstrate that anyone, even good Christians, can and have battled depression. You are not alone. Additionally, their experiences show that depression can have numerous and different triggers. For some, it may be a traumatic life event like death, destruction, or disease. For others, it may

3 C. H. Spurgeon, "Psalm 88 by C. H. Spurgeon," Blue Letter Bible, last modified December 5, 2016, https://www.blueletterbible.org/Comm/spurgeon_charles/tod/ps088.cfm.

be a prolonged season of great stress or anxiety. Still others may find themselves in depression because of discouragement, loneliness, disappointment, or anger. Sometimes depression swallows us when we've struggled to cope with life's inevitable changes, both physical and circumstantial. Even when external circumstances are satisfactory, internal circumstances can trigger depression. So, there is not just one reason for depression.

These examples also show us that depression is felt with many different symptoms. Some may feel intense sadness. Others may experience extreme loneliness and isolation. Still others may battle irrational anger, self-loathing, and grief. Depression can feel like a heaviness on the spirit, a stain on the soul, a dark cloud that threatens to rain on you at any moment. It can also come with symptoms of insomnia, constant exhaustion, listlessness, and lack of interest in anything that would normally excite or animate. Changed eating behaviors and even eating disorders may also be symptoms of depression. For many, it is a mixture of all the above.

Furthermore, these experiences of good Christians demonstrate that our symptoms of extreme sadness, sorrow, grief, fear, and anxiety may be valid. That is, they may be logical responses to real circumstances. For example, it is understandable that Job felt despair. He had lost everything dear to him and was covered in sores! However, that still does not make his conclusion—that it would have been better for him to have died at birth—true. While it is understandable that Elijah would feel discouraged and alone as he ran for his life with no help or companionship in sight, the fact was that God had hidden 100 other prophets who were also doing right (I Kings 18:4). From a human perspective, it makes sense that Jonah would be angry with God's plan for the people Jonah had hated so much. Still, this does not mean his conclusion—that God's plan was bad and that his own life was worthless—was correct. Likewise, David's sorrow over the success of his enemies was logical, but this doesn't mean his conclusion that God had abandoned him was true.

In other words, we may *feel* abandoned, but God has promised to never leave us or forsake us. We may *feel* lost in sadness, sorrow, or grief, but that does not mean we have to sink beneath the waves. We may *feel* like these battles will never end, but God promises to work all things together for the good of them that love Him. Our feelings are not the facts. They are *feelings*, and we must deal with them accordingly.

Now that we've diagnosed the problem, let's move on to what this book is about: ditching depression. If you can relate to the pig-tailed girl or C. H. Spurgeon or Job or David or any of the others, then you are in the company of good Christians who have wrestled and won the battle against depression. It's okay to admit you have a problem because that's the first step to finding a solution. A clearly defined problem is easier to solve. How wonderful that the Bible provides those solutions!

Part 2:
Ditching Depression

Chapter Three

The Proposition

The sun looked as if it were sinking into the silver sea, painting a pink and orange sky. The Atlantic Ocean was placid as two best friends–Jessica and Ryleigh–began reeling in their fishing lines. Neither of the girls had caught anything worth bragging about, but they had enjoyed each other's company. This was their favorite summer place–in a fishing boat, on the Atlantic, together. They chatted about past adventures and future dreams when Jessica noticed the wind picking up. Jessica's stomach flip-flopped as the waves picked up the boat and then dropped it down again.

"Getting choppy," Ryleigh said as she turned to check the boat motor.

At that moment, the waves rocketed the boat toward the sky, throwing Jessica far from the boat. Panicked, Jessica began flailing. The waves swept over her head and all she could hear was the sound of her heart throbbing in her chest. When her head bobbed above the water's surface again, Jessica searched left and right and to the sky as if to find a way of escape. Her stomach cramped, and her legs were already tired. Tears began to blur her vision. Was there no way out? Then a voice cut through the screaming in her brain. It was Ryleigh! Looking toward the sound of Ryleigh's voice, Jessica's weary body relaxed to see Ryleigh throw out a lifebuoy to her. Grabbing hold of the round, bobbing lifebuoy, Jessica knew she was safe. Gently, Ryleigh pulled her friend back toward the boat. After coughing up saltwater and shedding some tears, Jessica huddled near Ryleigh in the boat. Ryleigh looked down at Jessica and teased softly, "You were pretty stressed out. Forgot the lifeguard was on duty, huh?" Jessica responded with a nervous laugh. If only she had looked to Ryleigh first, she could have spared her body the extra anxiety and exhaustion.

Sometimes depression can be like an overwhelming ocean. Like Jessica, we frantically search for a way out, only to weary ourselves even more. In this stage, we may come to believe that there is no way to escape and place ourselves in a position to make harmful decisions. We've forgotten that there is a lifeguard on duty. God is our lifeguard, and He is always on duty. If only we will first look to Him for help, we can spare ourselves so much trouble.

The first step on our path to ditching depression is realizing that there is hope. If our Lifeguard is always on duty, then there is always hope for our situation. We can never say that there is no way out because God gave us a promise in I Corinthians 10:13:

> *There hath no temptation taken you but such as is common to man: but God is faithful, who will not suffer you to be tempted above that ye are*

> *able; but will with the temptation also make a way to escape, that ye may be able to bear it.*

This verse contains three key truths that will help us in this battle. First, we never face a temptation that someone else has not already faced. Our problem is not new. As we noted in the last chapter, several Bible characters struggled through seasons of depression and anxiety. Good Christians like C. H. Spurgeon have battled with depression and have had victory by God's grace.

Even more importantly, we cannot suffer something that Jesus Christ, our empathetic High Priest, cannot understand. Some well meaning people may say that they understand what we're going through when they really do not. But when Jesus says He understands what we are going through, He means it. Hebrews 4:15 says, *"For we have not an high priest which cannot be touched with the feeling of our infirmities; but was in all points tempted like as we are, yet without sin."* Because Jesus has already suffered the ultimate for us, He can empathize with our pain, whatever it may be. Jesus suffered just like we do. The only difference is that Jesus suffered perfectly; He never sinned. His suffering was never brought on by His sin because He had none. His suffering was brought on by our sin. And yet He still loves us and empathizes with us in our pain. What a comfort to know that though He is high and holy, Jesus has suffered for us and can empathize with us no matter what we experience.

A second key truth of I Corinthians 10:13 is that while we may go through trying experiences like depression, God has a good purpose in mind. Perhaps you are wondering why you, of all people, have struggled with depression. Maybe it seems like there is no logical reason for it. Take comfort in knowing that God has a purpose greater than your pain. He can turn ashes into beauty, and your struggle with depression is no exception.

The end of the verse says, *"that ye may be able to bear it."* God's purpose is to bring you *through* depression. He wants to bring you safely to the other side a stronger, more confident Christian. No matter how or why you have experienced this struggle, God is taking you somewhere.

The third key truth of this verse is that God has already made a way of escape. We know there is hope because God has already provided a way out of depression. The question is not whether God has provided a way of escape for you. The question is whether you are willing to take His way of escape.

This brings us to the second step we must take on this path to ditching depression. You must choose to take God's way of escape. This decision is not an easy, flip-a-switch change. Making this decision will not make all the physical and mental ailments of depression vanish overnight. While it is not an *easy* decision, it is a *simple* decision. We can make choices that do not align with our feelings, and we must, if we ever expect our feelings to change.

Here is the proposition: Choose to believe that there is hope and follow through on that belief by committing to a battle plan. This battle plan will be an intentional, comprehensive, and personalized strategy for fighting back against depression and anxiety. Since depression and anxiety are complex problems, and since human beings themselves are complex, this battle plan must be undergirded with biblical principles that address three battlefronts—the spiritual, mental, and physical. This is what it looks like to take God's way of escape from depression. Remember, there is a Lifeguard on duty, and He has a way of escape prepared for those willing to trust Him.

Chapter Four

The Spiritual Battlefront

While not every problem we face is a spiritual problem, every problem we face will affect us spiritually. God created us with a body *and* a spirit. The spirit is the immaterial part of us that can relate to God. Because everything we experience involves our spirits and our spirits are how we relate to God, the first battlefront on which we must fight is the spiritual front. The spiritual front simply refers to our personal relationship with the Lord.

Just like any relationship, our relationship with the Lord must be cultivated and nurtured through spending time with Him. We spend time with Him when we open His Word and talk to Him in prayer. Often, one of the first things to go when we are experiencing depression or anxiety is our daily time with the Lord.

During depression and anxiety, focus can be a struggle, and Bible reading and prayer both require focus. During these times, we may also feel that God is distant and aloof, making Bible reading and prayer seem like a stilted chore. To fight depression on the spiritual battlefront, we must take two important steps. We need to identify and deal with any spiritual contributors to our depression, and then we must cultivate our relationship with the Lord.

Identifying Spiritual Contributors to Depression

Unconfessed Sin

First, we need to consider some common spiritual contributors to depression. One such contributor could be unconfessed sin. Sometimes, the reason for this distant and awkward feeling may be that we have allowed sin in our lives. We should ask ourselves if there is any known sin hindering our relationship with God. As we discussed already, depression can have many different causes, and sin can be one of them. For example, allowing the sin of bitterness, unchecked anger, or envy to fester in our spirits can lead to depression.

This is not to say that sin is *the* cause of depression. Depression itself is **not** a sin any more than a physical sickness is sin. Hormonal imbalances are not sin. Feelings are not sin. How we respond to our feelings is what could become sin.

Still, sin can be a factor in depression. If sin is the cause of or primary factor in our depression, God will let us know what sin is hindering our relationship. God is not the author of confusion. Vague feelings of guilt and shame are not from God but from our enemy the devil. God does not shame us; He convicts us. Conviction means that we are convinced or persuaded that something is right or wrong. How can we be convinced if we don't know what that something is? If we can't think of a sin that could be inhibiting our fellowship with God, then we must not dwell there. If we do know about a sin that has broken our fellowship with God, then confession is the first step to spiritual healing.

In Psalm 32, David described the effects of known sin in his life. His song began with depression in verses 3-4: *"When I kept silence, my bones waxed old through my roaring all the day long. For day and night thy hand was heavy upon me: my moisture is turned into the drought of summer. Selah."* David paused to ponder the effects of unconfessed sin in his life. We see that David's silence about his sin took a physical and emotional toll on him. Perhaps you can relate. Maybe you know that you have been harboring bitterness in your heart, and it has led to physical sickness and depression in your life. Perhaps you have wronged someone else, and you have made no attempt to make things right. These sins can certainly lead to the inner turbulence and heaviness that David described in this psalm.

If you can relate to David, if you know of a sin that is stifling your fellowship with God, then confess it so fellowship can be restored. I John 1:9 says, *"If we confess our sins, he is faithful and just to forgive us our sins, and to cleanse us from all unrighteousness."* After we have confessed our sin, we may still feel guilt. Our enemy the devil wants us to feel trapped in our sin. But I John 2:1 continues, *"My little children, these things write I unto you, that ye sin not. And if any man sin, we have an advocate with the Father, Jesus Christ the righteous."* While the devil may be our adversary, Jesus Christ is our advocate. Whose testimony do you think is admissible in God's court? Take God at His Word when He says that confessed sin is forgiven.

Although David's psalm began with depression, it ended with joy because he rested in God's promise of forgiveness. In verse 5, David says, *"I acknowledged my sin unto thee, and mine iniquity have I not hid. I said, I will confess my transgressions unto the LORD; and thou forgavest the iniquity of my sin. Selah."* Notice that David paused again to ponder the promise of forgiveness. We too must dwell on God's forgiveness after we have confessed known sin in our lives. David left us with a challenge in verse 11, *"Be glad in the LORD, and rejoice, ye righteous: and shout for joy, all ye that are upright in heart."* Pondering God's promise of forgiveness brings gladness. Keeping short accounts with our Heavenly Father is an important part of spiritual healing.

Misconception of God

Perhaps sin has not initiated our depression, but another spiritual contributor, a misconception about God, has exacerbated our depression. Difficult circumstances can often distort our view of God. Seasons of difficulty can breed doubt in our minds about who we thought God to be. When God's actions toward us do not seem to match what we thought to be His character, cynicism may color our perspective.

This was the case for a woman named Naomi. The difficulty began with a famine in her homeland. In response to the famine, Naomi's husband transplanted the family to a forbidden and pagan land called Moab. Over a period of at least ten years in Moab, death robbed Naomi of her husband and her two sons. In despair, Naomi decided to return to her homeland of Judah. When her surprised neighbors welcomed her back home, Naomi insisted on being called Mara, *"for the Almighty hath dealt very bitterly with me"* (Ruth 1:20). She not only felt bitter over her losses, but she also *identified* as bitterness. How had she come to a point in her life where she had chosen a name for herself based on her bitter feelings? Naomi had allowed wrong assumptions about God and herself to take the wheel.

When her daughters-in-law pleaded to go with her to Judah, Naomi replied, *"it grieveth me much for your sakes that the hand of the LORD is gone out against me."* These words encapsulate at least two faulty assumptions Naomi had about God and herself.

First, she assumed that God was against her and that God's opposition to her had made her a menace to everyone around her. She felt like bad luck to her daughters-in-law. Surely, it would be better for them to return to their pagan gods than to remain with her and the God she assumed was against her.

Then, Naomi also made wrong assumptions about her future. As she told her tearful daughters-in-law, *"Turn again, my daughters, go your way; for I am too old to have an husband"* (Ruth 1:12). Naomi had lost all hope of experiencing love and provision again in her life, and she assumed that if her daughters-in-law accompanied her back to Judah, they would lose all hope of love and provision as well. All Naomi had to go on was her past experience. Her experience included sorrow and loss. She then took that experience and extrapolated it into the indefinite future, as if all that she could ever experience would be sorrow and loss. Naomi assumed that her story was over. You and I know, of course, that this was only chapter 1 of her story. *Hang on for another chapter*, we might urge Naomi, *and you'll see that redemption is coming!*

What about you and me? Have we allowed our experiences to distort our perception of who God is and how He acts in the world? While our experiences do affect us emotionally, we must not base our understanding of God on experience alone. We don't need to look in the rearview mirror, see a tragic past, and then allow faulty assumptions to drive us for the rest of the journey! We need to keep our eyes looking straight ahead at the next road-sign.

We must have the humility to realize that we don't fully know everything that is going on in our own lives. Naomi certainly did not know that she was about to be included in the story of King David of Israel—the royal ancestor of the Messiah. All she could see was famine, death, and destitution. To her, the future looked bleak. While this is an understandable human perspective, the Bible gives us a glimpse of God's perspective. Only God knows what is truly going on in our lives and, with Him, the best is always yet to come.

Like Naomi, when we think that our story is ending, it is only just beginning. As the apostle wrote in Romans 8:18, "*For I reckon that the sufferings of this present time are not worthy to be compared with the glory which shall be revealed in us.*" Ultimately, for every Christian, suffering is a temporary and fleeting prologue to the story God is writing for us. And it is a glorious story of joy, peace, purpose, and redemption that never ends!

So, let's take stock of our own perspectives about God. What are some lies that we may have swallowed? What are some characteristics we are attributing to God that contradict what Scripture says about God? Like weeds, these misconceptions can subtly take root in our hearts and choke out truths that once blossomed there. Uprooting these misconceptions is an essential step to spiritual healing.

Spiritual Warfare

Yet another potential contributor to our depression is spiritual warfare. Sometimes depression seems to hit us out of nowhere. No warning, no reasons, no preexisting conditions are in sight. In some ways, this may be the most difficult context for depression. When we feel it but we cannot understand *why* we feel it, we begin to wonder if there is a solution to it. As we mentioned with Naomi's story, we do not always know all the factors that are contributing to the circumstances of our lives. This is certainly true when it comes to the spiritual realm.

An example of this is the story of Job. You and I have read the beginning of the story where the devil approaches God with a request to persecute Job. However, Job did not know who or what was behind his horrifying circumstances. In Job 16:6, he cries out, *"Though I speak, my grief is not asswaged: And though I forbear, what am I eased?"* No matter what he said or did, Job could not find relief from his trial. And the worst part? He did not understand why it was happening.

While our circumstances may not be the same as Job's, we may have the same thoughts about our depression. We may have no clue *why* we are struggling so much and believe that nothing we do or say can make any difference. Ephesians 6:12 clues us into the realm we cannot see right now, saying, *"For we wrestle not against flesh and blood, but against principalities, against powers, against the rulers of the darkness of this world, against spiritual wickedness in high places."* This is the reason we are told to put on the whole armor of God. Just as the devil wished to destroy Job because he belonged to God, so the devil wishes to destroy us. Depression may be one of his tactics. But like Job, we can push back against the devil's assault.

The truth is that Job never did discover the conversation between God and the devil. However, Job kept his perspective upward. At times, he wallowed in his sorrow, but ultimately, he rested in what He knew about God—that God was just, sovereign, and good. Like Job, we must rest in the truth that God is just, sovereign, and good. If we do, then the depression will not win. We will be able to claim that victory that has already been won for us in Christ (I Corinthians 15:57). Spiritual warfare is real. The forces of darkness are strong. But the One who holds us is stronger (I John 4:4). The Lord says to us, "Look up, dear child."

Cultivating Our Relationship with God

After considering these spiritual contributors to depression, our next step to spiritual healing is cultivating our relationship with God. Like many other personal relationships, our relationship with the Lord may suffer during anxiety and depression. The last thing we may feel like doing amid depression is sitting down to spend time with the Lord. Yet that is what we need the most. Just like Jessica's calling out to Ryleigh was not a matter of virtue on her part, so our calling out to the Lord every day through Bible reading and prayer is not primarily a matter of being a good Christian. Like it was for Jessica, our calling out to the Lord is a matter of survival. When the waves of depression come crashing over our heads, we must not forget that there is a lifeguard on duty. Our daily time with the Lord is our lifeline in anxiety and depression.

Keep It Short & Sweet

We can maintain a daily time with the Lord when we implement three practical principles. The first is to keep our Bible reading short and sweet. While reading more of the Bible in one sitting is certainly a fine goal, it is not the ultimate goal. The ultimate goal is to get more of the Bible *into us* in one sitting. Ironically, this may require that we *read less* in one sitting and take more time to *meditate* on what we have read. When we are struggling with depression and anxiety, this is not the time to take on overwhelming goals like conquering the Bible in a year. Instead, we need to make the most of what little time and focus we may have.

A good place to start may be in the book of Psalms. Try reading a psalm a day and journaling what you learn about the character, attributes, and actions of God. Looking for something specific from your Bible reading can help improve focus and keep your thoughts on the Bible rather than feelings. If we are specifically struggling with misconceptions about God, we should make a list of things we currently believe about God and compare them to the list of attributes and actions of God that we find in the psalms. Over time, as we saturate our minds with God's Word, the fog of our misconceptions will give way to a clear view of God.

Keep It Simple

In addition to keeping it short and sweet, we must keep it simple. We should refrain from introspection—thinking deeply and analyzing our own feelings when reading a passage. To help guard against introspection, we may need to avoid devotional books or commentaries that deal heavily with feelings. While melancholy and pensive devotionals have their place, they are not helpful to a person living with depression. During depression, we do not need to read something that will match our mood. We need to read something that will challenge our mood. This may mean that we simply stick to reading just the Bible for a time. While many of the psalms share real, raw symptoms of depression, they do not leave us with that mood. They lead us to the one who can lift us. As David writes in Psalm 61:1-2, "*Hear my cry, O God; attend unto my prayer. From the end of the earth will I cry unto thee, when my heart is overwhelmed: lead me to the rock that is higher than I.*" Like David, we must look to the One who is higher than our mood and let Him lift us.

Keep Praying

Once we have made sure our Bible reading is short, sweet, and simple, we need to be in prayer. The prayer life we need does not look like mechanically marching through a prayer list. When we are struggling to maintain a daily time with the Lord because of depression, we must do what the psalmist did. In Psalm 62:8, David encouraged his people, *"Trust in him at all times; ye people, pour out your heart before him: God is a refuge for us."* As we have already seen from the several psalms we've read, David did not hold back his feelings. He told God exactly how he felt—every depressing, disgusting, disturbing detail.

Sometimes we think that we are so deep down in our dark hole that God couldn't possibly see us or want us anymore. David addressed this in Psalm 139:11-12, *"If I say, Surely the darkness shall cover me; even the night shall be light about me. Yea, the darkness hideth not from thee; but the night shineth as the day: the darkness and the light are both alike to thee."* Whether we are talking about physical darkness or emotional and mental darkness, the same principle applies. Our darkness is not dark at all to Him. God sees you and He *wants* you. The truth is that God already knows our hearts, but He wants to hear about it from us. Why? Because when we pour our hearts out to the Lord, we are inviting Him to intervene in our lives and demonstrating our dependence on Him.

Depression drains us of spiritual vibrancy. To revitalize our spirits, we need to deal with any spiritual contributors and cultivate our relationship with God through Bible reading and prayer. At first, these practices may feel like sheer acts of discipline. Yet as we continue in them, we will discover them to be the spiritual balm and nutrients that we have been craving. Our spiritual health is not just a matter of duty, but it is also a matter of survival. If we can win on the spiritual battlefront, we will have the fortitude we need to fight on the other two battlefronts as well.

Chapter Five

The Mental Battlefront

One of my favorite summer pastimes is getting lost on purpose. To me, true vacation is hopping in the car, taking some country roads, and choosing whatever turns I feel like. If I don't know where I am, maybe no one else does either. It's a liberating feeling. In the Cumberland hills of Tennessee, country roads are like incessant curves. One never quite knows what's around the bend until it is rounded, and then a whole new world appears. On these summer excursions, I've found dilapidated old farms, new farms teeming with grazing cows and horses, mountain views, historic battlefields, and little wide-spot-in-the-road towns I did not know existed. One just never knows where those country roads will lead, but it's usually to a beautiful and serene place.

Just like country roads in the Cumberland hills, thoughts are incessant curves in our minds that can take us to many places. Sometimes those places are exciting and colorful, sometimes beautiful and serene, and other times dark and scary. According to a recent study conducted by psychologists at Queen's University in Canada, over 6,000 thoughts whiz through our minds every day.[1] We are constantly thinking, even when we are unaware of it.

Identifying Negative Thought Patterns

Depression is characterized by overwhelmingly negative thoughts. Not only do depressed people think mostly negative thoughts, but they also ruminate on these negative thoughts, playing them incessantly in the mind. The brain becomes an echo chamber of these same negative thoughts. Even when circumstances are positive, these negative thoughts have already blazed trails through our brains, rendering us almost incapable of thinking accurate, logical, or positive thoughts about ourselves or our lives. During a depressive episode, we can be completely unaware of the fact that our thoughts are literally controlling our perspective, our emotions, and our life. Even when we know we have a good life circumstantially, our thoughts feed us negativity almost constantly. The negative thought patterns of someone living with depression could be categorized in several ways. Let's consider five common categories of negative thinking.

Oversimplified Thinking

In this pattern, our thoughts are like a pendulum swinging between extremes. Life is either completely great, or it is completely horrible. There is no realistic in-between. While life is a complexity of elements—some beautiful and others ugly—this depressive thought pattern does not recognize life's complexity.

1 J. Tseng, and J. Poppenk, "Brain meta-state transitions demarcate thoughts across task contexts exposing the mental noise of trait neuroticism," *Nautre Communication*, Vol. 11, No. 3480 (2020). https://doi.org/10.1038/s41467-020-17255-9.

Rather it simplifies all of life into the ugly category. Someone who has fallen into this negative thought pattern may have thoughts like this: "You messed up at work today. Can't you do anything right? This must mean that you are a complete failure!" If this depressed person does not get the job he interviewed for or the promotion he had hoped for, he may conclude, "You failed. You will never get anywhere in life." For this person, one mistake or perceived failure becomes the defining factor of his entire life. Because the depressed person did not meet some standard, whether real or self-imposed, he assumes that his life is a total failure. Often, goal-oriented people or perfectionists can fall into this negative thought pattern.

Negative Filter Thinking

As we said, life is a complexity of both beauty and difficulty. It is true that there is more than one way to look at any given situation, with some good and some bad to take away from it. However, this type of depressed thinking magnifies the negative and minimizes the positive.

A depressed person struggling with this kind of thinking may analyze every situation and say, "I feel so drained after that conversation. I must not be good with people. No one wants me around." Rather than considering the other reasons he might feel drained after a conversation, a depressed person filters out the positive and goes straight to the negative "reason" for the feelings he may be experiencing. Or he may think, "Every time I am given an opportunity to do something, I feel overwhelmed. I must be too weak to handle life." Instead of seeing opportunities, a depressed person dwells on his feelings of inadequacy and concludes that he cannot take those opportunities. Perhaps this depressed person receives some positive feedback on a project mixed with some criticism. This depressed person might completely ignore the positive and focus solely on the criticism. Even if the criticism is constructive, the depressed person will take it to mean he is no good. Dwelling on these negative feelings leads the depressed person to assume that his feelings of hopelessness or worthlessness are reality.

Prophetic Thinking

This is when something negative happens and the depressed person extrapolates that into the future. If a depressed person loses his job, he may think, "It always ends this way. I will never succeed in the workplace." Perhaps a depressed person gains back some weight that he worked hard to lose. He may conclude, "I gained the weight back. I'm so fat and I will always be fat!" Or perhaps after a close relationship suddenly ends, the depressed person trapped in this negative pattern will conclude, "You lost another friend. No one will ever love you! Why should they? What is there to love?" Extrapolating one negative experience into the future perpetuates this cycle of hopelessness. The depressed person becomes a self-fulfilling prophecy.

Topsy-Turvey Thinking

This thought pattern looks like taking positive comments or situations and interpretating them in the exact opposite way. This type of thinking looks at the world in a topsy-turvey manner. For example, upon receiving a compliment, a depressed person may reason, "They don't really mean it. They are just saying that because they feel sorry for me." Perhaps a depressed person gets a job promotion. Rather than accepting the congratulations, the depressed person may assume, "It's not really that big of a deal. I don't really deserve it anyway. They are just trying to patronize me."

Faulty Assumptions Thinking

This is when a depressed person makes assumptions about themselves or others based purely on feelings. For example, if a friend does not respond to a depressed person's text, he may assume, "He must not really want to talk to me. He hates me." Or perhaps when he is invited to help with a project, the depressed person assumes, "Don't even try. You know you can't do it." While there is no external evidence to confirm these conclusions, the depressed person assumes his feelings of worthlessness or inadequacy to be the facts.

Unrealistic Standards Thinking

This negative thought pattern consists of depressed people self-imposing certain standards on themselves and then berating themselves when they do not meet those standards. A depressed person thinks, "I should have gone to that party." Since he did not, he may think, "I'm such a terrible, antisocial person." Or perhaps a depressed person tells himself, "I should study for three hours tonight." Then when he fails to meet that standard, he thinks, "You're such a lazy loser!" Rather than realizing that he doesn't have to be at every party, the depressed person thinks that his absence means he is a bad person. Instead of viewing an hour of study as a success, the depressed person believes that he is lazy for failing to meet his high standard.

Blame Game Thinking

A depressed person often assumes that everything is his fault. When a friend is having a bad day and takes it out on him, a depressed person may think, "I must be a terrible friend. If I were a better friend, he wouldn't feel that way." Or when a friend quits his job, the depressed person assumes, "I should have supported him more. It's all my fault he's jobless." Whenever there is conflict or tension in a relationship or a negative outcome in a relationship, depressed people blame themselves for the tension or the negative outcome. Depressed people feel responsible for everything that goes wrong in their lives or the lives of those close to them.

Now, all of us have distorted thinking at times. Anyone may relate to any of these negative thought patterns. While negative thoughts can haunt all of us as human beings, depression is characterized by these thought patterns on a nearly constant basis. For the depressed person, these thinking patterns are not just a common occurrence; they are a habit. These thought patterns are not just a side-trip for the depressed person; they are the entire journey.

These thoughts may be illogical, irrational, and transparently false. Yet, when we are depressed, our minds are so programmed to think a steady diet of such negative thoughts that we don't know how to stop the flow. Thoughts that **do not** help to stop the flow but are often used to supplement are thoughts such as this:

"You should just toughen up!"

"You're just lazy. Snap out of it!"

"No wonder you have problems—you're not disciplined enough to do what you know you should do to help yourself!"

"You should be learning from your mistakes. It's your fault."

"You could just decide to do better next time, you know."

"Make yourself more lovable!"

"Do whatever it takes to please people, then maybe you'll have friends!"

"Just avoid anything that may be risky. Stick to what you know."

"Don't let people know much about you. The more they know, the more they can judge you."

Self-berating, self-deprecating thoughts like these will drive us further into our black hole. So, what is the solution to getting lost on these incessant curves of negative thought patterns? Instead of taking those same old trails that lead to dark places in our minds, we need to blaze new trails in our minds. Let's consider two steps toward that goal.

Blazing New Trails

Ask for Supernatural Help

The first thing we must do to blaze new trails in our brains is to ask Jesus to take our thoughts captive! Let's admit it—we cannot fight this battle on our own. Just as we cannot be stronger than the riptide when we swim against it, we cannot be stronger than the negative thought patterns when trying to take the steering wheel of our lives.

We must appeal to the supernatural power of the One Who created our minds in the first place. As the apostle Paul wrote in II Corinthians 10:3-4, *"For though we walk in the flesh, we do not war after the flesh: (For the weapons of our warfare are not carnal, but mighty through God to the pulling down of strong holds)."* As we learned earlier, the battle against depression is not just a physical battle. It is also a spiritual, emotional, and mental battle. This is not a fight we can go into with our fists or even our human reasoning.

We need something higher, greater, and much more powerful than ourselves to take back our thought life. The apostle Paul continues in II Corinthians 10:5, *"Casting down imaginations, and every high thing that exalteth itself against the knowledge of God, and bringing into captivity every thought to the obedience of Christ."* Depressive thoughts certainly are not obedient to Christ! They are run-wild-and-reek-havoc thoughts! God's Word says that you can't tame them, but Jesus Christ can.

When we feel a depressive episode seizing our minds, we should stop, drop, and pray! We can confess to Jesus that we don't have the power to overcome our depressive thoughts, admitting that our thoughts are rebellious, unruly, and wild. Then we can ask Jesus to cast them down. Pray that Jesus Christ would subject your thoughts to God's Word and that He would take them into captivity.

Once our thoughts have been captivated by Jesus, once our minds are fixed on Him, we can ask Him to renew our minds so that new thoughts can begin to blaze new trails in our minds. Ephesians 4:23-24 says, *"And be renewed in the spirit of your mind. And that ye put on the new man, which after God is created in righteousness and true holiness."* Because we are God's children, we have access to God's power on our behalf.

Our thought life can be characterized by righteousness and true holiness if we ask for God's renewal! Romans 12:2 exhorts, *"And be not conformed to this world: but be ye transformed by the renewing of your mind, that ye may prove what is that good, and acceptable, and perfect, will of God."* In this passage, the phrase *"renewing of your mind"* means "a renovation, complete change for the better that is affected by the Holy Spirit."[2] This means that we are not alone in this fight. The Holy Spirit which indwells us is there to renovate—to completely change—our minds. We can win the battle of the mind if we ask the Holy Spirit to take control and renew our minds.

2 "G342- anakainōsis- Strong's Greek Lexicon (kjv)," Blue Letter Bible, accessed April 26, 2022. https://www.blueletterbible.org/lexicon/g342/kjv/tr/0-1/

Filter and Replace Our Thoughts

What characterizes a mind under the Holy Spirit's renovation or renewal?

A renewed mind filters out wrong thoughts and replaces them with right thoughts. From II Corinthians 10:5, we learn what we are *not* to be thinking. Now, let's look at what we *are* to be thinking. Philippians 4:8 gives us quite a list: *"Finally, brethren, whatsoever things are true, whatsoever things are honest, whatsoever things are just, whatsoever things are pure, whatsoever things are lovely, whatsoever things are of good report; if there be any virtue, and if there be any praise, think on these things."* Our thoughts must be filtered through Philippians 4:8.

The first filter through which we are to put our thoughts is truth. Are we thinking on what is true? Often, depressive thoughts of hopelessness stem from misconceptions about ourselves and about God. An example of what is *not* Philippians 4:8 thinking would be Naomi in Ruth 1:13 when she told her daughters-in-law, *"It grieveth me much for your sakes that the hand of the LORD is gone out against me."* Because Naomi's past experience was filled with famine, sorrow, and loss, she assumed that her life would always be that way and that God was against her. When we put this through the truth-filter of Philippians 4:8, we find that it does not pass the test. The truth which contradicts this thought is found in the promise that God will never abandon us (Hebrews 13:5) and that even when he chastens, He does so in love, not in opposition to us (Hebrews 12:6). Like in Naomi's case, if our thoughts are not true, then neither can they be honest, just, pure, lovely, virtuous, or of good report.

We must keep in mind that Philippians 4:8 is not a list of types of thoughts we should think. It is an entire system of thinking. Philippians 4:8 is to be a filter through which we put every thought. If it does not pass all the requirements, then it is not a Philippians 4:8 thought. For example, if a thought is true, but it is not also lovely, then we are not to ruminate on that thought. If a thought is lovely, but it is not honorable or excellent, then we are not to dwell on it. Filtering our thoughts through Philippians 4:8 may sound tedious, but there are several habits that can help us do just that.

Journaling

When a depressive episode has us drowning in negative, wrong, unlovely, untrue thoughts, it's extremely difficult to think clearly enough to sort the true from the untrue. One thing that can help with that is journaling. When thoughts are hitting us like a tidal wave, we can channel that wave through a pen and onto paper. Writing down every nasty, ugly little thought helps to get them outside our heads and in a place where we can actually face them. When we do this, we begin to see how wrong and often irrational depressive thoughts are. They often sound much more reasonable in our heads, but when we can see them on paper, we can more easily sort the true from the false and the lovely from the unlovely.

Contrasting Thoughts

Once we have reached the point where we discard our thoughts as contradictory to Philippians 4:8, we are ready to replace them with counterthoughts. One way we can do this is by jotting down our thoughts on one side of a 3x5 card or piece of paper, and then writing down God's thoughts with a Scripture reference on the other side. How do the thoughts that we feel are true about us and our lives compare with the thoughts God says are true about us and our lives? Perhaps we could create a Philippians 4:8 thought chart like the one below.

Your Thought	*God's Thought*	*Scripture Support*
"My life is worthless."	"You are my precious creation and my priceless child."	Psalm 139:14, "I will praise thee; for I am fearfully and wonderfully made: marvelous are thy works; and that my soul knoweth right well." Matthew 10:30-31, "But the very hairs of your head are all numbered. Fear ye not therefore, ye are of more value than many sparrows."
"No one could love me."	"I have always loved you and nothing will change that. I have proven this to you over and over again."	I John 4:9, "In this was manifested the love of God toward us, because that God sent his only begotten Son into the world, that we might live through him." Romans 8:38-39, "For I am persuaded, that neither death, nor life, nor angels, nor principalities, nor powers, nor things present, nor things to come, Nor height, nor depth, nor any other creature, shall be able to separate us from the love of God, which is in Christ Jesus our Lord."
"I have no future. I have nothing to offer the world."	"I am writing your story. I have a plan and I will perform it. I can give through you to the world."	Psalm 138:8, "The LORD will perfect that which concerneth me: Thy mercy, O LORD, endureth for ever: Forsake not the works of thine own hands." Jeremiah 29:11, "For I know the thoughts that I think toward you, saith the LORD, thoughts of peace, and not of evil, to give you an expected end."

Your Thought	*God's Thought*	*Scripture Support*
"I can't do this. I can't go on. I should just give up."	"In my strength, you can always do the right thing. In your weakness, I am strong."	John 16:33, "These things I have spoken unto you, that in me ye might have peace. In the world ye shall have tribulation: but be of good cheer; I have overcome the world." Philippians 4:13, "I can do all things through Christ which strengtheneth me." II Corinthians 12:9, "And he said unto me, My grace is sufficient for thee: for my strength is made perfect in weakness."
"I'm all alone. I'm going to die alone."	"You are never alone. I am with you."	Joshua 1:9, "Have not I commanded thee? Be strong and of a good courage; be not afraid, neither be thou dismayed: for the LORD thy God is with thee whithersoever thou goest." Matthew 28:20, "Lo, I am with you alway, even unto the end of the world." Hebrews 13:5, "For he hath said, I will never leave thee, nor forsake thee."

*In the back of the book, you will find a blank chart that you can fill out for yourself.

The next time a depressive episode engulfs us, we can refer to this chart or 3x5 cards and read God's truth back to ourselves. The benefit of having these truths on 3x5 cards is that we can carry them with us wherever we go and use them as needed throughout the day. Over time, we will retrain our minds to dwell on Philippians 4:8 thoughts.

Keeping a Happiness Jar

Gratitude—we hear about it a lot in modern wellness and self-care culture. Popular social media posts about becoming the best version of yourself always prescribe the obligatory gratitude journal as part of a daily routine. Even secular health professionals are talking about the benefits of practicing gratitude. For example, psychotherapist Amy Morin says that gratitude improves our physical health, psychological health, and mental strength, among other benefits.[3] What our culture may classify as a novel scientific discovery is simply the way that God designed us to be.

God designed us in such a way that gratitude *helps us*. Sometimes we assume that since gratitude should be about giving God thanks and glory (and it should), then it must be purely a spiritual discipline which makes us good Christians. However, God commands us to practice gratitude not only because He is worthy of it, but also because it is essential to our spiritual and mental health! God will be glorified whether we thank Him or not. But He calls us to gratitude because it helps us to recognize God's hand in our lives. While it may sound cliché, it is true that those who seek for God in their life will find Him.

A creative way to count our blessings is by creating what we might call a Happiness Jar. We can do this by writing down anything good that happens or any blessings in our lives. They may be as big as financial provision or an answer to prayer, or they may

---

3 Amy Morin, "7 Scientifically Proven Benefits of Gratitude That Will Motivate You to Give Thanks Year-round," *Forbes*, November 23, 2014, forbes.com/sites/amymorin/2014/11/23/7-scientifically-proven-benefits-of-gratitude-that-will-motivate-you-to-give-thanks-year-round/?sh=486f0217183c.

be as small as a smile that made us feel special or a good cup of coffee. Whatever good things we find, we write them down on a piece of paper and toss it into our happiness jar. Then, the next time depression seeks to drag us under, or anxiety begins to constrict our chest, we can start taking those pieces of paper out and reading them one by one. The depressive thoughts may be relentless, but we will be ready to counter them with God's blessings in our lives. Reading them out loud can make this practice even more effective. This action will not only keep our minds busy so that the depressive thoughts can't take over, but it will also train our minds to think on the positives in our lives.

Restricting Social Media Use

Several years ago, I deleted my Instagram account and I've been much happier ever since. Now, I haven't cut social media completely out of my life. I still have accounts on a couple platforms that I barely use. Before I deleted Instagram, I was beginning to feel that it was taking up more of my time and mental and emotional energy than was healthy. After doing some research, I found that my experience was in no way abnormal.

According to Statista, 82% of the U.S. population in 2021 were social media users.[4] A 2021 Pew Research report found that 71% of Americans ages 18-29 say they use Instagram, while 65% of Americans ages 18-29 say they use Snapchat. Facebook and Youtube still have the most users among social media platforms.[5] Most Facebook, Snapchat and Instagram users say they visit

---

4 S. Dixon, "Percentage of U.S. Population who currently use any social media from 2008 to 2021," Statista, July 7, 2022, https://www.statista.com/statistics/273476/percentage-of-us-population-with-a-social-network-profile/.

5 Brooke Auxier and Monica Anderson, "Social Media Use in 2021," Pew Research Center, April 7, 2021, https://www.pewresearch.org/internet/2021/04/07/social-media-use-in-2021/.

these social media sites daily. These statistics demonstrate that social media has a significant influence in the daily lives of many Americans. Social media has its tentacles in everything! Even one of my Bible apps has the option to add friends and frequently recommends people I may know from my contacts. I've often rolled my eyes, thinking, "I don't want to socialize on my Bible app; I just want to read the Bible! Is nothing sacred?" After a few years of distance between myself and my personal Instagram account, I began to realize how it had affected my mental health.

What about you? What is your experience with social media? After an hour of scrolling on social media, do you usually feel more fulfilled, content, and happy? Or is the reverse true for you?

Whether you've thought about it or not, the influence of frequent social media use on our mental health has been in question for a while. A recent study found a causal link between frequent social media use and anxiety and depression.[6] Researchers in this study monitored a group of 143 undergrad students at the University of Pennsylvania for three weeks. These students were randomly separated into two groups. The experimental group was limited to 10 minutes on three social media platforms, amounting to 30 minutes a day on social media. The other group had unlimited access to social media. At the end of the study, those in the experimental group who had started with the greatest levels of depression reported the greatest decline in depression. While a study like this does not reveal the reasons for the causal link between social media and anxiety and depression, we can probably make some educated guesses.

---

6 Gigen Mammoser, "The FOMO Is Real: How Social Media Increases Depression and Loneliness," *Healthline*, December 9, 2019, https://www.healthline.com/health-news/social-media-use-increases-depression-and-loneliness#Our-curated-lives.

One reason frequent social media use can harm our mental health is that it breeds comparison and envy. Social media opens a whole new world to us, giving us access to more intimate details about more people than we were ever meant to have. This overload of knowledge shoves comparison in our faces. We automatically size ourselves up next to that young woman who just posted a selfie. We measure our career success according to the job promotion that he just posted. We are content with our lives until we get a glimpse into someone else's lifestyle, or at least the one he projects on social media. We enjoy our own family until we see that mom post her latest "Day in the Life" video. According to clinical psychologist, Rachel Andrew, "What social media has done is make everyone accessible for comparison. In the past, people might have just envied their neighbors, but now we can compare ourselves with everyone across the world."[7] But we don't need a psychologist to tell us that social media can stoke envy in our hearts.

Have you ever had that sinking feeling in your stomach after scrolling through Instagram and seeing a classmate or a casual acquaintance tout their latest vacation, job promotion, or relationship? With a whole world now open for us to compare ourselves to, self-pity, self-loathing, envy, and covetousness become magnified problems.

Not only does social media give us access to the entire world for comparison, but it also gives us access to the burdens of the whole world. While it is good to be informed on national and world events, we were not built to bear the burdens of the entire world on our shoulders. The constant news cycle makes us constantly aware of all the evil that is happening in the world.

---

7 Moya Saner, "The age of envy: how to be happy when everyone else's life looks perfect," *The Guardian*, October 9, 2018, https://www.theguardian.com/lifeandstyle/2018/oct/09/age-envy-be-happy-everyone-else-perfect-social-media.

In addition to this awareness, we feel the pressure to comment on current events as if we are experts. Anyone with social media can be an expert, and most act as if they are, posting about current events, social controversies, and politics with certain hashtags. Seeing such posts makes us feel like we also must comment on the world stage. We must have a stance on the issue, and we must make it known. We are required not just to care about everything but to say and do something about everything. We feel this responsibility to fix the world, and when we cannot fix it, we feel like we have failed the world. The problem is that . . . well, we are not God! Only God has the capacity to know about, care about, and do something about everything that goes on in the world.

This concoction of comparison to others and the save-the-world complex plays a major role in the feelings that lead to chronic anxiety and depression. We can't sleep because the last thing we look at before we go to bed is the news and people's response to that on social media. A better nighttime routine for our mental health would be to make the Bible app rather than the Twitter app the last thing we look at before bed. Yes, we are called to bear one another's burdens (Galatians 6:2), but we are also called to cast all our cares upon Him (I Peter 5:7). We are told to care about, pray for, and help others, but we are also to take all of that care and ultimately entrust it with Jesus. We are not in control, but He is. Rather than spending most of our time scrolling through the outrage and backlash on social media, we should spend more time praying for our friends, neighbors, church, city, and state. Our mental health will be better for it.

When I deleted my Instagram account, I didn't think it would make that much of a difference on my mental health. While it wasn't the only factor that improved my mental health, it played a much bigger role than I thought it would. I'm not saying that everyone should delete their Instagram accounts too! I'm simply saying that if you can relate to any or all of these feelings, maybe you should consider at least restricting your social media use.

Social media, like any other technological tool, can be a great force for good. We can use it to connect with more people worldwide. We can build online communities based on similar interests or stages in life. Anyone anywhere can build a platform on which to influence, inspire, and exhort others. Yet when we go from being the user to the used, social media can wreck our mental health. The difference maker is being extremely intentional about our social media use so that it is a tool which works for us, rather than a leech that sucks the very peace, joy, energy, and life out of us.

So, how is your relationship with social media right now? Is your social media use helping you in this battle for your mind or hindering you? These are personal questions that only you can answer. Don't be afraid to answer them and make changes accordingly. The battle for your mind is more important than anything you think you may be missing by decreasing or deleting social media.

Winning on the mental battlefront is essential. If we don't make the necessary changes there, we cannot expect our feelings and symptoms to change. Taking these steps toward mental healing will aid us in our efforts on the next battlefront—our physical well-being.

Chapter Six

The Physical Battlefront

In Psalm 102:4, the psalmist laments, *"My heart is smitten, and withered like grass; so that I forget to eat my bread."* Amid his intense suffering, Job cried, *"For my sighing cometh before I eat, and my roarings are poured out like the waters. For the thing which I greatly feared is come upon me, and that which I was afraid of is come unto me. I was not in safety, neither had I rest, neither was I quiet; yet trouble came"* (Job 3:24-26). In their distress, these two men could not bring themselves to do something as simple as eating. Their distress was not only emotional and mental but physical as well.

Depression may be caused by physical infirmities or accompanied by physical infirmities, or sometimes depression may cause physical infirmities. Depression may also lead us to the neglect of our bodies. Either because we are so overcome with sadness or because we feel utterly underserving of care, we may neglect our physical needs or even inflict harm on ourselves.

When we are mired in depression, we may neglect to care for our bodies in simple ways. Self-neglect may look like binge eating and then groaning on the couch followed by days of restricted eating. It could look like not eating enough, not eating at all, or eating only one type of food. Another way depression may lead us to neglect ourselves is by sleeping too much. Sleep can be a sweet escape from depression, and sometimes depression drains us of our will to get out of bed, take a shower, and get ready for the day. Why put effort into making ourselves look nice when we feel awful? On the other hand, depression may lead us to neglect sleep altogether, either because we cannot sleep or because we won't allow ourselves to sleep. Whatever form it takes, neglecting to care for our bodies can lead to greater physical problems.

Sometimes self-neglect may escalate to self-harm. Self-harm is deliberately hurting oneself to relieve emotional pain without the intention of suicide. Feelings of guilt, grief, or self-loathing could drive someone to self-harm. Sometimes self-harm is used to manage emotions or give the person a sense of control in what he perceives to be an otherwise out-of-control life. For some, it is a form of penance or something to break up the monotony and emotional numbness that usually plagues them. Self-harm provides an adrenaline rush, stimulation, and a physical pain to counter the emotional pain that is tormenting the person. However, this relief doesn't last for long. For this reason, the self-harm can become an addiction.

Whether through inflicting pain, ingesting drugs, or simply neglecting the body's basic needs, self-harm is not God's design for us. What does the Bible say about self-harm? We see several places in the Bible where self-harm is portrayed in a negative light. I Kings 18:24-29 describes the worshippers of Baal cutting themselves as part of their religious ritual. Their self-harm did not yield an answer to their earnest prayers. The maniac of Gadara cried out and cut himself because of spiritual oppression. Jesus put an end to his self-harm when he cast out the demons and restored the man to his right mind. When Paul and Silas saw the

Philippian jailer pointing a sword toward his chest, they cried out, *"Do thyself no harm"* (Acts 16:28). As a result, the Philippian jailer accepted Christ as his Savior. From these passages, we see that self-harm is not pleasing to God and that Jesus is the primary solution to this problem.

Even if we have never practiced self-harm, we may have neglected our bodies because of depression. Contemplating self-harm or neglecting our physical well-being grieves the Lord just as much as actively inflicting harm on our bodies. If we are going to have victory on the physical battlefront, we must first have a biblical perspective of our bodies.

Biblical Perspective of the Body

Which is more important to God—our spirit, mind, or body? Okay, that was a trick question. The answer is yes. Christianity is unique from other worldviews in that it equally values both the material and immaterial part of human beings. Secular religions, such as atheism or humanism, purport that matter is all there is and emphasize self-love and self-care above all else. Traditional Eastern religions view the body as unimportant and emphasize neglecting or even abusing the body to liberate the soul. In contrast to either extreme, God cares about the whole person He created which includes both the spiritual and physical parts.

God's Creation

Since God cares about our bodies, we should think the way He does about them. First, we need to view our bodies as God's precious creation. Genesis 1:26-27 says,

> *And God said, Let us make man in our image, after our likeness: and let them have dominion*

> *over the fish of the sea, and over the fowl of the air, and over the cattle, and over all the earth, and over every creeping thing that creepeth upon the earth. So God created man in his own image, in the image of God created he him; male and female created he them.*

We bear the image of God Himself! This means that we are like God in some ways and that we are to represent God's character to the world around us. Fulfilling this purpose includes our whole body. While God could have spoken us into existence, God took special care in designing the human body. Genesis 2:7 tells us that God created Adam by forming him out of the dust of the ground. In other words, God created the human body in love and detail. This is true, not just for Adam, but for every human being born since then. We see this idea in Psalm 139:13-16,

> *For thou hast possessed my reins: thou hast covered me in my mother's womb. I will praise thee; for I am fearfully and wonderfully made: marvelous are thy works; and that my soul knoweth right well. My substance was not hid from thee, when I was made in secret, and curiously wrought in the lowest parts of the earth. Thine eyes did see my substance, yet being unperfect; and in thy book all my members were written, which in continuance were fashioned, when as yet there was none of them.*

Yes, human beings are created by the natural processes that God ordained, but He is still intimately involved in the creation of every human body. Just as an artist has the right to do what he wants with his creation, God has the right to do what He wants with our bodies. They are His creation.

God's Possession

Second, we need to view our bodies as God's sacred possession. If you are a believer, not only have you been lovingly created by God, but you have also been graciously redeemed by God. In a sense, you are doubly owned by God. I Corinthians 6:19-20 says,

> *What? Know ye not that your body is the temple of the Holy Ghost which is in you, which ye have of God, and ye are not your own? For ye are bought with a price: therefore glorify God in your body, and in your spirit, which are God's.*

God is emphatic about His possession of our bodies in this passage! He says, "*which ye have **of God** . . . ye are **not** your own . . . ye are **bought** with a price . . . which are **God's**.*" This passage teaches that we are God's sacred, meaning set-apart, possessions, paid for with an exorbitant price. God gave us the bodies He wanted us to have. We gave our bodies over to sin, but God has bought them back with the blood of His own Son! Because they are doubly owned by God, our bodies are to be used for His purposes. We have these bodies on loan from God for a time that He has appointed. If we had a house on loan, would we burn it to the ground or allow it to fall apart? Of course not! So, why would we then harm our bodies or let them deteriorate when we have them on loan from God? Clearly, we have no right to do so. Since we are the dwelling place of the Holy Spirit, we are to glorify God in our spirits *and* in our *bodies*, which are *God's*.

God's Purpose

In addition to viewing our bodies as God's creation and possession, we must also understand that our bodies have eternal purpose. Not only has God created and redeemed our bodies, but He has also promised to restore our bodies to His original design. Because of Christ's resurrection, a resurrection and restoration of our physical bodies is coming. The bodies we have right now are corruptible, but they will be resurrected and transformed into incorruptible bodies. I Corinthians 15:51-53 says,

> *Behold, I shew you a mystery; we shall not all sleep, but we shall all be changed, in a moment, in the twinkling of an eye, at the last trump: for the trumpet shall sound, and the dead shall be raised incorruptible, and we shall be changed. For this corruptible must put on incorruption, and this mortal must put on immortality.*

This resurrection and restoration have always been part of God's grand redemptive plan, as verses 54-57 state:

> *So when this corruptible shall have put on incorruption, and this mortal shall have put on immortality, then shall be brought to pass the saying that is written, Death is swallowed up in victory. O death, where is thy sting? O grave, where is thy victory? The sting of death is sin; and the strength of sin is the law. But thanks be to God, which giveth us the victory through our Lord Jesus Christ.*

God created our bodies for life, not death. Although sin threatened to ruin that purpose, God has given us victory over sin and death through Christ's death and resurrection. Right now, we are being conformed to the image of Christ, in a spiritual sense. Someday, we will have bodies like Jesus' glorified body. As Philippians 3:20-21 says,

> *For our conversation is in heaven; from whence also we look for the Savior, the Lord Jesus Christ: who shall change our vile body, that it may be fashioned like unto his glorious body, according to the working whereby he is able even to subdue all things unto himself.*

If God has planned a resurrection for our bodies, why would we treat our bodies as if they were bad or worthless? A glorious future awaits our physical selves as well as our spiritual selves. No wonder God commands us to glorify Him in our spirit *and* in our bodies which doubly belong to Him!

Now that we have a biblical perspective of our bodies, we can glorify God in the way that we steward our bodies. How can we glorify God in our bodies when we are mired in depression and anxiety? We can glorify God in our bodies when we take care of them so that they can be used in God's service. Two primary ways we can fight successfully on the physical battlefront are by reestablishing routine and reaching out to others.

Reestablishing Routine

Often one of the first things to suffer when depression hits is a daily routine. Depression makes difficult even the most basic decisions, like when to wake up or go to bed or if and when to eat. Life becomes a series of random events, thrust into motion by our own chaotic feelings. As humans, we thrive when we have purpose and actionable steps that push us toward that purpose.

Since we can't rely on ourselves to make the right decision in the moment, we need a pre-planned and scheduled routine. This takes the guesswork out of our day. Let's consider three basic things that should be included in our routine.

Sleep

We live in a culture that devalues sleep. Often, college students or workaholics will brag about how little sleep they've gotten. But sleeplessness is not a virtue like courage or diligence. Sleeplessness can be a severe detriment to our health physically, emotionally, mentally, and spiritually. You've probably heard someone say, "We'll sleep when we're dead." The truth is if we don't sleep, we will be dead sooner than we may have thought.

While this may sound hyperbolic, sleeplessness is linked to a host of health issues, including depression. According to the Sleep Foundation, "Depression and sleep issues have a bidirectional relationship. This means that poor sleep can contribute to the development of depression and that depression makes a person more likely to develop sleep issues. This complex relationship can make it challenging to know which came first, sleep issues or depression."[8] In their book about sleep and brain function, three researchers cite several studies that suggest, "Sleep complaints often precede the onset of depression and constitute an independent risk factor in the development of the disorder."[9] Inadequate sleep can be both a symptom of depression as well as a causal factor in depression. The reason sleep deprivation

---

8 Rob Newsom and Alex Dimitriu, "Depression and Sleep," Sleep Foundation, accessed December 16, 2022, https://www.sleepfoundation.org/mental-health/depression-and-sleep.

9 Peter Meerlo, Robbert Havekes, and Axel Steiger, "Chronically restricted or disrupted sleep as a causal factor in the development of depression," *Sleep, Neuronal Plasticity and Brain Function* (2015): 459-481.

can trigger or worsen depression is that it disrupts our brain function.

While we sleep, our brain encodes memories, including emotional memories. When our sleep is consistently disrupted, our brain's emotional processing is impaired.[10] One study observed two control groups—one with proper sleep and another with sleep deprivation—and found that the sleep control group encoded "a balanced mix of both positive and negative memories" while the deprivation group had a "skewed distribution, finishing the encoding session with an overriding dominance of negative memories."[11] Furthermore, the results of this study indicated that sleep deprivation impairs our ability for "next-day emotional learning."[12] In simpler terms, when we do not sleep, we do not store up as many good emotional memories as we do bad, which in turn causes us to pick up more negative emotions the next day.

These studies demonstrate that developing a healthy sleep habit is not optional when it comes to our mental health. Healthy sleep habits are collectively called sleep hygiene, indicating that sleep is just as basic and foundational to health as eating your vegetables or brushing your teeth. When creating a sleep schedule, we should consider three essential elements.

---

10 Matthew P. Walker and Els van der Helm, "Overnight therapy? The role of sleep in emotional brain processing," *Psychological Bulletin*, Vol. 135, No. 5 (2009): 731-48, dio: 10.1037/a0016570. https://www.ncbi.nlm.nih.gov/pmc/articles/PMC2890316/?__hstc=52210678.7e8615a5748130a197e122153bfa1faf.1487289600051.1487289600052.1487289600053.1&__hssc=52210678.1.1487289600054&__hsfp=528229161

11 Ibid.

12 Ibid.

Consistency

First, we need to keep a consistent sleep schedule. This includes being consistent with the *number of hours* we sleep per night and the *time we wake up and go to bed* each day and night. According to the CDC, teenagers need 8-10 hours of sleep per every 24 hours and adults need 7 or more hours per night. While sleep needs vary, most people need about 7-8 hours of sleep per night.

We should build our sleep schedule around the number of hours we need every night. For example, if we need to sleep 8 hours per night, then we should set a bedtime and wake time that will allow us those 8 hours. If we do not prioritize the number of hours we sleep, we can fall into sleep debt! According to the Sleep Foundation, sleep debt "is the difference between the amount of sleep someone needs and the amount of sleep they get."[13] Maybe you get to bed half an hour late one night and then lose an hour of sleep the next night, another half hour the next night, and then two hours the next night. This means that you are now four hours in sleep debt, and your body will demand that you pay it back! Studies have shown that while a person may not feel sleepy because of sleep debt, his cognitive and physical performances will decline.[14] If we are already in sleep debt, recovering those lost hours may take days or even weeks.

To recover from sleep debt, we must slowly increase the amount of time we sleep by increments of 15 to 60 minutes each night.

---

13 Rob Newsom and Dr. Anis Reham, "Sleep Debt and Catching up on Sleep," Sleep Foundation, last updated March 1, 2023, https://www.sleepfoundation.org/how-sleep-works/sleep-debt-and-catch-up-sleep.

14 Hans P. A. Van Dongen, et al, "The cumulative cost of additional wakefulness: dose-response effects on neurobehavioral functions and sleep physiology from chronic sleep restriction and total sleep deprivation," *Sleep* Vol. 26, No. 2 (2003): 117-26. doi:10.1093/sleep/26.2.117, https://pubmed.ncbi.nlm.nih.gov/12683469/

Over time, our bodies will recover from sleep debt. The best policy, of course, is to avoid getting into sleep debt.

Equally important to sleeping a set number of hours is consistently *going to bed* and *waking up* at the *same times* every day. Our circadian rhythm is our body's internal clock that regulates our sleep-wake cycles. Our circadian clock, as we might call it, picks up on environmental cues such as the light in the daytime and dark in the nighttime to regulate our wakefulness and sleepiness. When our circadian clock is thrown off by sleep disturbances or unhealthy sleep habits, this can lead to sleep disorders like insomnia.

According to the Sleep Foundation, one factor that can contribute to throwing off our body's natural rhythm is "delayed sleep phase disorder."[15] This is when someone habitually stays awake late into the night or early morning and then sleeps later in the morning and during the day. Since this should be avoided, we should retrain our bodies to sleep when it is sleep time (night) and wake up when it is wake time (morning). If your job requires you to stay up later and sleep in later, then at least strive to maintain a consistent bedtime and wake time. *The time of day or night* we sleep does matter, but if that element cannot be controlled, then sticking with our set bedtime and wake time is key. As we are consistent, our circadian rhythm will do what God created it to do—regulate a healthy sleep cycle.

For most people, it takes more discipline to go to bed at the same time every night than it does to get up at the same time every morning. While we have pressures to get us up in the morning, going to bed at night is often left to us. This is the reason that

15 Eric Suni and Alex Dimitriu, "Circadian Rhythm," Sleep Foundation, last updated February 16, 2023, https://www.sleepfoundation.org/circadian-rhythm.

setting a consistent sleep schedule should begin with setting a hard rule about bedtime. If we can be consistent with going to bed on time, we have already won half the battle for good sleep hygiene.

Nighttime Routine

Another aspect of sleep hygiene is developing a nighttime routine. Since our circadian clock is influenced by our environment, it is important that we create an environment conducive to a regular sleep cycle. For example, at least thirty minutes before bed, we should dim the lights and avoid electronic devices. The light from our phones and laptops interferes with our body's circadian rhythm. The key is to avoid activities that will excite our minds or stimulate our bodies. For example, watching the news, scrolling through social media, or doing vigorous exercise right before bed should be avoided.

Additionally, we can signal to our bodies that it is sleep time by relaxing the mind and muscles. This may mean that we include stretching in our nightly routine. Maybe you need to take a walk and a hot shower an hour before bedtime to release the day's pent-up tension. Perhaps keep a book on the nightstand for reading with a cup of tea before bed. This can help the minds to stop dwelling on all the worries and cares of the day and focus on something pleasant before bed.

Sometimes our bodies are tired, but our minds won't let us get sleepy. If this is a struggle, taking sleep supplements may help. For example, melatonin is the body's natural hormone that promotes sleepiness, but you may need to take a melatonin capsule if your body is not releasing enough melatonin. Perhaps consult a nutritionist about other natural sleep supplements that may help your body regulate sleepiness. Drinking herbal teas that promote sleepiness may also be a safe and helpful option.

Planning for Restlessness

In addition to staying consistent with our sleep schedule and nighttime routine, our sleep hygiene should include a plan for combatting restlessness. Getting to sleep may feel like an accomplishment, but sometimes staying asleep is the bigger accomplishment. If you are struggling with depression, restless sleep may be a problem for you. Don't let it defeat you! Have a plan so that you can be in control in those moments. Maybe you should have a book ready to read, an activity ready to do, or a funny show ready to watch. Read your Bible or quote Scripture from memory over and over in your mind. Drink tea or eat a healthy snack. Get out your 3x5 cards and read God's thoughts about you. Instead of counting sheep, start counting your blessings from your happiness jar. Having a plan for those sleepless nights will help to guard against depressive episodes.

Over time, having a consistent sleep schedule, nighttime routine, and plan for restlessness will train our bodies to sleep properly. While our modern culture may not value sleep, God commands us to take care of our bodies. Sleep is a vital part of that.

Remember when Elijah fled for his life into the wilderness and begged God to take his life? His physical exhaustion played a major role in his depression. What did Elijah do after his desperate wish for death? He slept! What did he do when he woke up? He ate and drank, and that sustenance renewed his strength. Sometimes the most spiritual thing we can do is sleep, eat, and drink. Eating and drinking is what we will look at next.

Nutrition

Another foundational element to our physical health is our diet. Diet does not mean a trendy weight loss program. It just refers to our eating habits. A healthy diet is one that includes the vitamins and minerals our bodies need to function.

Many Americans are deficient in certain vitamins and minerals because the foods they eat have been depleted of those vitamins and minerals. Especially when battling depression or anxiety, the temptation is to eat too much, too little, or not at all. We also tend to grab the wrong foods for comfort when dealing with depression. Grabbing highly processed foods like junk food or fast food can compound the problem. Highly processed foods can lead to inflammation in the body, which in turn can heighten depression and anxiety.

Basic nutrition has been shown to aid in recovery from depression and anxiety.[16] While there are no magical foods that cure depression, some foods have been shown to reduce depression. Foods which improve intestinal health have been linked to mental health as well. According to the American Psychological Association, intestinal bacteria are responsible for most of our body's production of serotonin—the hormone that stabilizes mood and affects feelings of well-being and happiness.[17] Such foods would include yogurt and other fermented foods, avocado, whole grains, leafy greens, and lean proteins.

Some vitamins have also been linked to helping relieve depression. For example, *omega-3 fatty acids* are linked to enhancing brain function and improving mood. Foods rich in

16 F.N. Jacka, A. O'Neil, and R. Opie, et al, "A randomised controlled trial of dietary improvement for adults with major depression (the 'SMILES' trial)," *BMC Med* Vol. 15, No. 23 (2017), https://doi.org/10.1186/s12916-017-0791-y https://bmcmedicine.biomedcentral.com/articles/10.1186/s12916-017-0791-y

17 Siri Carpenter, "That Gut Feeling," *Monitor on Psychology,* Vol. 43, No. 8 (September 2012): 50, https://www.apa.org/monitor/2012/09/gut-feeling#:~:text=Gut%20bacteria%20also%20produce%20hundreds,both%20mood%20and%20GI%20activity.

omega-3 fatty acids would include salmon, tuna, walnuts, and flax seeds. Another vitamin that has been linked to reduced risk of mood disorders is vitamin B, specifically *B-12 and B-9*. Eggs, dairy, and poultry are good sources of vitamin B-12. Vitamin B-9 (folate/folic acid) can be found in leafy dark green vegetables, beans, and whole grains. Some studies have shown that *zinc* helps to lower depression.[18] Good sources of zinc would include nuts, beef, and whole grains. Eating in moderation from every food category provides the various vitamins our bodies need to function.

If you are deficient in any of these vitamins, you might consider taking vitamin supplements. For example, if you do not prefer eating fish, you may consider taking an omega-3 vitamin supplement. Do your research to discover what foods you might be lacking in your diet. Create a meal plan that will make grocery shopping and mealtime less stressful while also providing you with essential nutrients. Perhaps you should consider getting help from a nutritionist to establish a supplement regiment and meal plan. When we give our bodies these essential vitamins and minerals, we are being good stewards of the bodies God gave us.

Exercise

Like sleep and nutrition, exercise is basic to our overall health. However, studies have shown that exercise is an effective treatment for depression and is often just as effective as medication or therapy.[19] Whether someone's depression is

---

18 T. S. Sathyanarayana Rao, et al., "Understanding nutrition, depression, and mental illness," *Indian Journal of Psychiatry*, Vol. 50, No. 2 (2008): 77-82, https://www.ncbi.nlm.nih.gov/pmc/articles/PMC2738337/.

19 Lynette L. Craft and Frank Perna, "The Benefits of Exercise for the Clinically Depressed," Primary care companion to the *Journal of Clinical Psychiatry*, Vol. 6, No. 3 (2004): 104-111, https://www.ncbi.nlm.nih.gov/pmc/articles/PMC474733/.

caused by chemical imbalance, stress, or inflammation in the body, exercise can help to relieve any of these problems. One reason is that exercise releases chemicals called endorphins into our brains. These feel-good chemicals relieve stress and help the body cope with pain. Exercise also increases the release of chemicals like serotonin and dopamine to our brain. As we mentioned earlier, serotonin is the hormone that stabilizes our feelings of well-being and happiness. Dopamine is a chemical messenger in the brain that, when released in large quantities, can produce feelings of pleasure. Exercise can also improve our sleep quality—a double strike against depression.

So, how can we implement exercise into our battle plan?

Time

First, we need to decide what days and what times we will exercise. Most medical sources recommend 150 minutes of exercise per week.[20] That could be broken down into thirty minutes, five days a week, for example. If exercise is new for you, then make three days a week your initial goal. Once you have decided which days of the week you are going to exercise, decide what time you are going to exercise each day. Does morning exercise work for you or is evening exercise better? After a long day at work, muscles are tight and the mind is tired. The benefit of exercising in the evening is that it helps relieve the tension and stress of the day, making the body relaxed and ready to wind down for the night. Exercising in the morning can also be beneficial as it helps to energize our bodies for the day. Experiment to discover what agrees with your body and best fits your schedule.

20 "How much physical activity do adults need?" Centers for Disease Control and Prevention, Physical Activity, accessed June 2, 2022, https://www.cdc.gov/physicalactivity/basics/adults/index.htm.

Type

Next, we need to select the types of exercise we will do each time. If your exercise plan is to be sustainable, it should include exercises you enjoy. Maybe you enjoy running, swimming, hiking, or brisk walking. Biking is a great aerobic and strength training exercise. Perhaps there is a sport you enjoy playing, like volleyball, basketball, soccer, or tennis which you could make part of your weekly exercise routine. Maybe walking for fifteen to thirty minutes a day could be the place to start. Wherever you are right now and whatever you choose to start with, give yourself grace and just commit to moving every week. As you begin to try different types of exercises, you will discover what you enjoy and what makes your body feel its healthiest and strongest. Eventually, creating an exercise routine that includes both aerobic and strength training will be beneficial for both mind and body.

Place

Finally, it is important to consider where we exercise. Make sure you have a place that you can easily access. For example, you could create a space for exercise at home. Perhaps you could make an extra bedroom or a den into your exercise space. Better yet, take your exercise outside in God's creation. Exposure to sunshine increases—you guessed it—serotonin levels. Studies have shown that just five minutes of exercise in nature can improve our mood and self-esteem.[21] There's just something about God's creation! We were meant for movement, and we were meant to enjoy the nature God created. So, get a good

---

21 Jo Barton and Jules Pretty, "What is the best dose of nature and green exercise for improving mental health? A multi-study analysis," *Environmental Science and Technology,* Vol. 44, No. 10 (2010): 3947-55, https://pubmed.ncbi.nlm.nih.gov/20337470/.

dose of vitamin D and fresh air while you drink in the scents, sounds, and sights of nature.

As we have considered the way God designed our bodies, we can see that taking care of our bodies through sleep, nutrition, and exercise is foundational to our overall well-being. If we are going to glorify God in our bodies, that will require intentionality in these three areas. All three should be included in our routine. Self-care in these three areas is not selfish; it is a stewardship. We are caring for something that belongs to God but is entrusted to us—our bodies.

Reaching Out to Others

In addition to reestablishing routine in our lives, we need to be reaching out to other people. Amid depression, our tendency is to retreat, hibernate, and hide from other people. Depression may be accompanied with social anxiety or simply a lack of motivation for human interaction. However, giving into these anti-social tendencies is the worst thing we could do for our depression. God created us as social and relational beings. While some of us may be more introverted than others, we all need other people in our lives. God calls us to love one another and to bear one another's burdens. Let's look at two specific ways we can do that.

Project People

At one point in my struggle with depression, my dad assigned project people to me. I made a list of friends, family, and neighbors and acts of kindness I could do for them. One of those neighbors was an elderly widow. Although I did not feel like doing anything or seeing anyone at the time, I baked banana bread and took it to her on a cool spring day. The visit turned into a lengthy conversation. While my depression was not cured from one visit, it was relieved. The visit allowed my mind to change channels, even if only for a few minutes. The more time I spent intentionally looking for ways to help other people, the more natural it became. Over time, this helped me to realize that other people cared about me and needed me. Likewise, I came to realize just how much I cared about and needed others. God created us to be mutually beneficial to each other. We care for and need each other!

The project people strategy helped me battle depression because it is based on a Bible principle. The principle of putting others first is woven throughout the entire Bible. Philippians 2:4 says, *"Look not every man on his own things, but every man also on the things of others."* In Romans 12:10, Paul wrote, *"Be kindly affectioned one to another with brotherly love; in honor preferring one another."* The idea behind the phrase, *"in honor preferring one another"* is that of esteeming others highly and deferring to them. Later in Romans 15:2, Paul exhorts, *"Let every one of us please his neighbor for his good to edification."* While we could go on, these verses already demonstrate that God expects us to be kind to, care for, and encourage others.

When we are told to put others first, we often object, "How can I help other people if I need help? How can I help others be okay if I'm not okay?" That is a valid question. Another principle we see sprinkled throughout the entire Bible is that God blesses obedience. He takes care of those who trust and obey Him. When praising a church for their generous giving to him, Paul wrote, *"But my God shall supply all your need according to his riches in glory by Christ Jesus"* (Philippians 4:19). The psalms are also filled with promises for those who trust in God and obey His commands. Psalm 37:3 says, *"Trust in the LORD and do good; so shalt thou dwell in the land, and verily thou shalt be fed."* The promise is that when we look beyond our own problems to the things of others, God will make sure that we are taken care of also. You don't have to wait until you are better to help others because that is part of the process God is using to make you better.

Another reason the project people strategy works is that it destroys one of the common lies depression tells us. Often depression whispers in our ears that we are useless or that other people would be better off without us. Helping others decimates that lie and renews that sense of usefulness, purpose, and connection with others. God created us in such a way that helping others is helping ourselves.

So, make your own list of project people. The projects can be as simple as giving a smile or a hug, sending a text message, or sending a note to someone. Your project could be giving a gift or helping someone with a job. As you look out for other people, you will find that God looks out for you.

Accountability Partner

A second way that you can be reaching out to others is by asking someone to be your accountability partner. This is especially important if you are struggling with a more severe depression. An accountability partner should be godly, trustworthy, and spiritually mature. This could be a pastor or pastor's wife, a friend, or a family member. Telling someone else about your depression is not easy, but it is important to let at least one godly, trustworthy, mature person know what is going on in your life. It's good to hear someone you trust say that they love and are praying for you. Your accountability partner can also help you create your battle plan, incorporating the spiritual, mental, and physical aspects. Then they can help you walk through the process, keep you on track, and remind you to have patience and give grace to yourself. Perhaps you can set up regular coffee dates, walks, or some other meeting arrangement that will work for your schedules.

The truth is none of us were meant to do life alone. Reaching out is not a sign of weakness. In fact, it takes more courage and strength to reach out than to retreat in self-isolation. When you take that step, you will find that you are not alone in your struggle, that you are needed, and that you are very loved. God can use other people to heal you. Psalm 147:3 says, *"He healeth the broken in heart, and bindeth up their wounds."* Let someone who loves you be part of God's healing process for you.

Tying It All Together

Christianity doesn't simplify human beings into one-dimensional beings. The Bible does not treat people as simply material bodies or entrapped souls. Rather, Christianity treats human beings as the complex image-bearers of God that they are, composed of both spiritual and physical parts. Since human beings are complex, depression is a complex issue. Some may experience depression because of a psychological issue, while others may experience it because of a physiological or emotional issue. Whatever the cause and whatever the factors, the Bible addresses depression from all angles. The Bible gives us the tools we need to fight back on the spiritual, mental, and physical battlefronts. When we make and use our comprehensive battle plan, we can ditch depression. Then, we will be ready to discover joy again.

Part 3:
Discovering Joy

Chapter Seven

The Object of Joy

On our journey back to joy, two questions become apparent. What is joy, and where can we find it? One dictionary definition of joy is "a deep feeling or condition of happiness or contentment." One of the Bible words for joy often used in the New Testament means "a calm delight." Both these definitions speak of an inner condition, not a superficial feeling.

When we say we want joy, we mean we want something more than just surface-level, fickle happiness. We want something nestled within our souls that is not so easily moved. And joy is not just a feeling—it's a state of being, a condition. While feelings fluctuate easily, it takes much more work and intention to change a condition. How do we obtain this deep condition of happiness that we call joy? When we are on the journey to discovering joy, the first step is identifying the object of our joy. The object of our joy is whatever we look to for that deep feeling of happiness or condition of contentment. Our joy will only be as good as the object of our joy.

The Object of Self

The search for joy is an age-old one, and there are several common objects of joy. One common object of joy is self. Some will say that the only way to overcome self-loathing is to commit to self-love. Our inner wrestling would cease if only we could love ourselves more. According to Dr. Jeffrey Bornstein, "Self-love is a state of appreciation for oneself . . . Self-love means having a high regard for your own well-being and happiness. Self-love means taking care of your own needs and not sacrificing your well-being to please others. Self-love means not settling for anything less than what you deserve."[1] Some examples he offers of practicing self-love include, "Talking to and about yourself with love, prioritizing yourself, and trusting yourself."[2]

In an article declaring different women's definitions of self-love, one woman described it like this: "You look in the mirror and you remind yourself how amazing and loveable you are." Another said, "We need to first love ourselves to truly give love to others, too." A third woman explained, "Self-love means freedom . . . and reminds me that, 'Girl, you need to take a little more for yourself." Yet another woman said, "No one can perform self-love for you, so it's important to be your own best friend."[3] Based on these definitions and descriptions, self-love is looking within yourself for the answers, confidence, and care you need to combat depression and find joy.

---

1 Jeffrey Borenstein, M.D., "Self-Love and What It means," *Brain and Behavior Research Foundation*, February 12, 2020, https://www.bbrfoundation.org/blog/self-love-and-what-it-means.

2 Ibid.

3 Natalie Lusinki, "11 Women Describe Exactly What Self-Love Means to Them," *Bustle*, July 27, 2018, https://www.bustle.com/p/11-women-describe-exactly-what-self-love-means-to-them-9910840.

The culture of self-love says that if we are not happy, we must simply look inward, tap into our hidden potential, and draw out our true selves. Our true selves are pure, flawless, and beautiful. We can trust our true selves. We can ditch depression and discover joy, if we reject everything and everyone that is hindering us from fully following our hearts and doing what seems right to us.

Let's put the object of self-love to the test of God's Word. Can self-love be an adequate object of joy? When we look for the words self and love in the Bible, they do not appear together in the same way that they do in our self-love culture. In Matthew 22:37-40, we see the words love and self together in what have been called the two greatest commandments. Here Jesus says,

> *Thou shalt love the Lord thy God with all thy heart, and with all thy soul, and with all thy mind. This is the first and great commandment. And the second is like unto it, Thou shalt love thy neighbor as thyself. On these two commandments hang all the law and the prophets.*

Notice, the first great commandment is not "Love thyself." Neither is the second great commandment an admonition to "take a little more for yourself." However, the underlying assumption found in the second great commandment is that we do love ourselves. This kind of self-love is a natural awareness of ourselves, our needs, and our desires. This basic self-love is necessary for survival and thriving. What this kind of self-love does not include is an obsession with ourselves, our needs, and our desires. Rather than starting with self, Jesus' commandments start with God and then other people. Every other of God's laws hinges on this imperative to love God with our whole being and love others. We are not told to love ourselves in order that we may love others. We are told to love others in the way that we naturally love ourselves. That is, we should seek to be aware of their needs and desires and treat them with the grace, mercy, and understanding we want to receive ourselves.

Based on this cursory study of the two greatest commandments, it would seem that our modern understanding of self-love inverts Jesus' priorities in Matthew 22:37-40. If I wait to love others until I have learned to fully accept and like myself, I may be waiting forever. Focusing on making myself feel better about myself will only drive me further into the hole of self-deprecation and self-defeat. While God certainly wants me to like and accept the person He has made me to be, He does not want me to prioritize liking myself. God does not intend for us to obsess over accepting ourselves or fixate on pleasing ourselves. Instead, God created us to operate in such a way that when we love God and pour love into others, we ourselves are filled with love.

To love God and others the way we ought, we must remember that we are already fully loved. I do not have to like everything about myself to be loved because I am already fully loved by God. Romans 8:38 says,

> *For I am persuaded, that neither death, nor life, nor angels, nor principalities, nor powers, nor things present, nor things to come, nor height, nor depth, nor any other creature, shall be able to separate us from the love of God, which is in Christ Jesus our Lord.*

When I am secure in God's love for me, I am free to love others as Christ loved me. I don't need to worry about loving myself when I've accepted that God already loves me with a perfect love. I John 4:18 says, *"There is no fear in love; but perfect love casteth out fear: because fear hath torment. He that feareth is not made perfect in love.*" When we believe in and rest in God's perfect love for us, that love perfects us. It matures us. One sign of that maturity is the absence of fear—fear of our own unworthiness and God's judgment. As I mature in God's love, I am released from the need to love myself because I am already loved perfectly.

Fundamentally, the reason self-love is not an adequate object of joy is that we cannot look to the source of our problem to also be the solution to our problem. What do self-loathing and self-love have in common? They both begin with *self*. Rather than looking to ourselves for love, we must look to our Creator Jesus Christ. C. S. Lewis said it like this:

> Look for yourself, and you will find in the long run only hatred, loneliness, despair, rage, ruin, and decay. But look for Christ and you will find Him, and with Him everything else. [4]

The Object of Circumstances

Another common place people look for joy is circumstances. Circumstances are what happen to us and what happens around us. *Happ*iness, by definition, is connected to what *happens* to us and around us.

Think of several things that have happened in your life. Perhaps getting your first bicycle comes to mind. Maybe you think of your graduation day, wedding day, or the birth day of your first child. Buying your first house or getting an unexpected promotion

4 C.S. Lewis, *Mere Christianity*, (New York, NY: Harper Collins, 2001), 227.

at work may spring to mind as well. When you think of these happenings, it brings a smile to your face. They conjure good, warm, happy feelings. That is as it should be. But maybe you have also remembered falling off your bicycle and scraping your knee. Your mind may bring up the time you failed an exam, lost a job, or lost a loved one. These happenings wipe the smile from your face and stir feelings of sadness, loss, and maybe even anger. From this little thought experiment, it is apparent that happiness is a fine thing to want; it is a normal human emotion connected to circumstances. Circumstances are up and down, and so is our happiness.

But is happiness the same thing as joy? As we've already discussed, joy includes happiness, but it is also more than happiness. Joy is that deep condition, that contented state of being, that inner calm delight. So, can circumstances be the source of joy?

The prophet Habakkuk understood that circumstances were an inadequate object of joy. During a time of God's judgment, Habakkuk's circumstances were far from happy. He looked around him and saw his nation in a state of spiritual depression. The fulfillment of prophesied judgment—Babylonian captivity—was imminent. Habakkuk certainly could not smile and laugh away the reality of the desolate fig tree, the fruitless vines, the failing olives, the withering fields, or the scattered livestock around him. In Habakkuk 3:18-19, the prophet declares,

> *Yet I will rejoice in the LORD, I will joy in the God of my salvation. The LORD God is my strength, and he will make my feet like hinds feet, and he will make me to walk upon mine high places.*

Habakkuk's joy was rooted in something less volatile than what was happening to him or around him. Amidst changing circumstances, Habakkuk was rejoicing in the LORD, whose character and attributes never change. Habakkuk found life, joy, and strength in God. Just like the deer frolics over hills because God sustains his life, so Habakkuk knew that he could go through life with joy because God would sustain him.

Similarly, the apostle Paul testified to the fact that he could not rejoice in his circumstances but in the God sovereign over his circumstances. In Philippians 4, the apostle Paul describes that contented state of being when he says,

> *Not that I speak in respect of want: for I have learned, in whatsoever state I am, therewith to be content. I know both how to be abased, and I know how to abound: every where and in all things I am instructed both to be full and to be hungry, both to abound and to suffer need.*

Paul had experienced highs like being called a god and lows like being stoned and left for dead. But his joy remained constant. Our lives can feel like roller coasters—sometimes we are up and sometimes we are down. But life doesn't have to be a joyless ride if the object of our joy is not our circumstances.

The Object of Others

Yet another common object of joy is other people and our relationships with them. While we are commanded to love others, we are not commanded to find our joy in others. This is not to say that other people and our relationships with them cannot nurture joy. In fact, your relationship with your spouse *should* nurture joy. You should rejoice over precious friendships and budding relationships with your children. Finding happiness and comfort in a strong connection to your parents is natural. The point is not that we should not enjoy our relationships; the point is that we shouldn't make our relationships the sole source of our joy.

Much like circumstances, relationships with other people can change. Often changes are the result of two people in the relationship changing, but sometimes the change is inexplicable. The problem with making people the object of our joy is that they cannot live up to our standards. For example, if a woman looks to her husband as the source of her joy, then she will grow resentful of him when he does not deliver on her expectations. Similarly, if a father depends on his child to bring him joy, he will become disappointed when the child does not accomplish the father's hopes and dreams for the child. People and relationships change; people can let us down. But our joy does not have to devolve with devolving relationships. David wrote in Psalm 27:10, "*When my father and my mother forsake me, then the LORD will take me up.*" And that brings us to the relationship that *can* source our joy. Let's consider the object of joy which actually allows us to enjoy other things like our circumstances and relationships.

The Object of Christ

We have already been picking up clues along the way as we've looked at inadequate objects of joy. Self-love looks to the source of the problem to solve the problem—an obvious issue. Circumstances are an unstable source for joy. Relationships change and therefore make for an insecure object of joy. In comparing each of these inadequate objects to the Bible, the same source has shown up again and again—God.

In Matthew 22:37-40, Jesus commands us to love God with our whole being because He is the only worthy object of such love. In God, we live and move and have our being, so it follows that loving Him would bring us joy! In Habakkuk 3, the prophet realized that God's salvation and strength was the only sure thing—the only sure source of joy.

Likewise, the apostle Paul encouraged his friends in Philippi to, "*Rejoice in the Lord alway: and again I say, Rejoice.*" Notice Paul did not say, rejoice in your circumstances. The verse doesn't say, "Rejoice in the good things of life." It doesn't say rejoice in your clothes or your food or a place to sleep. It doesn't say rejoice in your health or your wealth. If that were what the verse said, then what would we do when even those things are taken from us? What if we don't have clothes, food, or health? Then what would we have to rejoice in? No, the verse says to rejoice in the *Lord*.

Ultimately, the Lord is the only and best object of our joy and rejoicing. Rejoicing is the outward expression of our inward condition. Rejoicing in the Lord doesn't mean you are smiling or laughing all the time. Rejoicing in the Lord doesn't mean that you feel happy all the time or that you must pretend that nothing is ever wrong. Rejoicing in the Lord means meditating on Jesus and what He has done in saving your soul rather than meditating on earthly things. Rejoicing in the Lord means talking about God's good character: His unmatched holiness, His fathomless greatness, His unmerited lovingkindness, His infinite wisdom, and His undying compassion for His people.

From Philippians 4, we also see that joy is not first and foremost a feeling. At first, joy is a choice. Paul doesn't say, "Feel joyful in the Lord." He commands us to "Rejoice in the Lord." It's an action. Paul ends his letter to the Philippians with a very familiar verse: *"I can do all things through Christ which strengtheneth me."* We are used to seeing this verse pasted on Christian sports jerseys or inspirational Instagram posts, but what is it really about? Within the context of Philippians 4, it is about kicking self-pity. It's about choosing joy. We can *choose* to rejoice in the Lord *through Christ* who strengthens us!

When we choose joy, that joy in turn strengthens us to live in a way that pleases God. While depression sucks the life out of us, joy restores our strength. Nehemiah 8:10 says, *"The joy of the LORD is your strength."* Christ's joy is what keeps us going even when self, circumstances, and other people let us down. Even when our feelings of happiness fluctuate, joy is like the personal flotation device that keeps us afloat in the sea of life. When we are resting in joy, just like we would rest in a flotation device, we will not be taken under by those threatening waves of depression.

In our journey to discovering joy, we must start with the correct object. What is the object of your joy right now? Is it self? Is it circumstances? Is it other people? I think C. S. Lewis eloquently sums up this section on the object of joy:

> What Satan put into the heads of our remote ancestors was the idea that they could 'be like gods'—could set up on their own as if they had created themselves—be their own masters—invest some sort of happiness for themselves outside God, apart from God. And out of that hopeless attempt has come nearly all that we call human history—money, poverty, ambition, war, prostitution, classes, empires, slavery—the long terrible story of man trying to find something other than God which will make him happy. The reason why it can never succeed is this. God made

> us; invented us as a man invents an engine. A car is made to run on petrol, and it would not run properly on anything else. Now God designed the human machine to run on Himself. He Himself is the fuel our spirits were designed to burn, or the food our spirits were designed to feed on. . . . God cannot give us a happiness and peace apart from Himself, because it is not there. There is no such thing.[5]

It makes sense that the One who created us is the only One who could fulfill us. God created us for Himself. While our selves, circumstances, and relationships may be unstable, God is our Rock. If Christ is the object of our joy, then we must nurture our personal relationship with Him. That is why we are going to consider some ways to cultivate our joy in the Lord.

5 C. S. Lewis, *Mere Christianity*, (New York, NY: Harper Collins, 2001), 50.

Chapter Eight

Cultivating Joy

Now that we have looked at the object of our joy, let's consider how we can cultivate our joy in the Lord. To cultivate something means to promote or improve the growth of something. Just as a farmer must take time and intentionality to care for his crops, so we must take time and intentionality to promote and improve the growth of joy in our lives. Throughout the Bible, we see several Christian disciplines that can cultivate our joy in the Lord.

Prayer

One way to cultivate our joy in the Lord is staying connected to Christ through prayer. Prayer is our direct line of communication to God. When we pray, we are simply asking God for something, demonstrating our dependence on His power and goodness.

Prayer is something that Jesus taught His disciples to do while He was on this earth, but it was also something He told them to continue doing even after He would leave this earth. Knowing that his death, resurrection, and ascension were imminent, Jesus delivered a farewell address to his disciples in John 16. He explained that while He would not always be with them physically, they could stay connected to Him through prayer. In John 16:24, Jesus told his disciples, *"Hitherto have ye asked nothing in my name: ask, and ye shall receive, that your joy may be full."* Prayer cultivates joy in our lives!

So, how is prayer supposed to work?

The book of Psalms gives us many examples of prayer. In Psalm 5, we see David's goal in prayer, the content of his prayer, the direction of his prayer, the time of his prayer, and the result of His prayer. In verses 1 and 2 David says, *"Give ear to my words, O LORD, consider my meditation. Hearken unto the voice of my cry, my King, and my God: for unto thee will I pray."* David's goal in prayer was to get God's attention. He boldly sought audience with God while also recognizing God's authority over his life. David addressed God as "my King, and my God," submitting to His authority. The content of David's prayer was simply his meditation—what he was thinking about, the burdens of his heart. Likewise, when we pray, we should not think of it as simply a spiritual exercise. We should pray with the goal of getting God's attention. We should pray in recognition and submission to God's authority. And we should pray about what is on our hearts.

These verses also tell us the direction and time of David's prayer. Verse 3 continues, *"My voice shalt thou hear in the morning, O LORD; in the morning will I direct my prayer unto thee, and will look up."* The direction of David's prayer was upward and the time of his prayer was early. Rather than looking within himself for the answers, David directed his prayer to God, and he did so in the morning before the hurries and worries of the day could infringe on his time with the Lord. As David did, we should direct our prayer to God at the start of our day. This will put us in a posture of prayer throughout the entire day.

Now what is the result of David's prayer? The psalm ends like this:

> *But let all those that put their trust in thee rejoice: let them ever shout for joy, because thou defendest them: let them also that love thy name be joyful in thee. For thou, LORD, wilt bless the righteous; with favour wilt thou compass him as with a shield.*

Prayer is the ultimate expression of our trust in God. And God blesses those that trust in Him with favor, protection, and joy.

One reason prayer cultivates joy is that, while we wait on the Lord in prayer, we learn more about His character and promises. Another psalm of prayer, Psalm 130, begins with depression: *"Out of the depths have I cried unto thee, O LORD."* However, this psalm ends with hope because waiting on God is always worth it: *"My soul waiteth for the Lord more than they that watch for the morning: I say, more than they that watch for the morning."* Psalm 130:3-4 highlight God's good character, saying, *"If thou, LORD, shouldest mark iniquities, O Lord, who shall stand? But there is forgiveness with thee, that thou mayest be feared."* Similarly, verse 7 says, *"Let Israel hope in the LORD: for with the LORD there is mercy, and with him is plenteous redemption."* No matter the depths from which we may be crying to Him, we can have hope and joy in waiting when we dwell on the mercy, forgiveness, and redemption of God.

Then, Psalm 130:5 highlights hope in God's promises, saying, *"I wait for the LORD, my soul doth wait, and in his word do I hope."* While waiting on God may not be something we would choose, it provides an opportunity to learn about, claim, and *pray* the promises of God. What are some promises that you need to claim during your season of waiting? God promises that His grace is sufficient in our weakness (II Corinthians 12:9). He promises that every experience can be used for our good, to conform us to the image of his Son (Romans 8:28-29). We are promised peace when we set our minds on Him (Isaiah 26:3). He promises to provide for our needs if we seek Him first (Matthew 6:33, Philippians 4:19). We are promised clear guidance when we delight in God and commit our way to God (Psalm 37:4-5). God promises to finish what He starts in our lives (Philippians 1:6). We are promised the filling and power of the Holy Spirit when we truly thirst for and ask for Him (Luke 11:13). God promises victory over sin through our faith in Jesus Christ (I John 5:4). There are so many promises for the Christian to claim in prayer!

Prayer cultivates joy not only because we learn about God's character and promises but also because we can see God act in our lives! In Psalm 116:1-2, David exclaims,

> *I love the LORD, because he hath heard my voice and my supplications. Because he hath inclined his ear unto me, therefore will I call upon him as long as I live.*

In verse 7, David says, "*Return unto thy rest, O my soul; for the LORD hath dealt bountifully with thee.*" David did not just learn more about God's character and promises; he experienced God in a real and personal way. The joy that prayer produces comes not just from receiving things that we need or want but from seeing God show up in our lives. As we commune with God in prayer, we begin to not only know about Him but experience Him in real life. There is nothing more invigorating for your spiritual life than seeing God answer your prayers! The only way to see that happen is to start praying. As David did in Psalm 5, make the meditations of your heart the prayers of your mouth.

Purity

Another way to cultivate joy is through pursuing purity. Pursuing purity is a twofold responsibility. One aspect of pursuing purity is refraining from sin and asking God's forgiveness when we do sin. Earlier, we considered David's experience with the devastation that sin brings into a life. In Psalm 51, he confesses to God his sin with Bathsheba, and asks in faith for the restoration of joy that comes with a pure heart. In verses 7-12, David writes,

> *Purge me with hyssop, and I shall be clean: Wash me, and I shall be whiter than snow. Make me to hear joy and gladness; that the bones which thou hast broken may rejoice. Hide thy face from my sins, and blot out all mine iniquities. Create in me a clean heart, O God; and renew a right spirit within me....Restore unto me the joy of thy salvation; and uphold me with thy free spirit.*

But pursuing purity is about more than just refraining from doing things that displease God. Pursuing purity is about actively doing that which pleases God. We are happiest when we are doing good works because that is the entire purpose for which we were saved in the first place. Titus 2:14 says that Jesus "*gave himself for us, that he might redeem us from all iniquity, and purify unto himself a peculiar people, zealous of good works.*" Similarly, Ephesians 2:10 says, "*For we are his workmanship, created in Christ Jesus unto good works, which God hath before ordained that we should walk in them.*" So, how can we do these good works that purify our lives?

In John 15, Jesus continues His farewell address to his disciples, saying in verses 4 and 5,

> *Abide in me, and I in you. As the branch cannot bear fruit of itself, except it abide in the vine; no more can ye, except ye abide in me. I am the vine, ye are the branches: He that abideth in me, and I in him, the same bringeth forth much fruit: for without me ye can do nothing.*

Abiding in Christ means recognizing Him as our power to do right. It means trusting Christ. Just as it was by faith in Christ's work that we were saved, it is by faith in Christ's work that we can produce good fruit in our lives. When we ask Christ for the strength to do right, we can actively pursue good works which in turn cultivates our joy. As Jesus says in verses 10-11, *"If ye keep my commandments, ye shall abide in my love . . . These things have I spoken unto you, that my joy might remain in you, and that your joy might be full."* The formula Jesus gives in this passage is simple: trust Christ's strength and obey His commandments. If we do this, Christ's joy in us will remain and be full!

Praise

Yet another way to cultivate our joy in the Lord is through praise. The Bible tells us to pray without ceasing, but it also commands us to praise without ceasing! Remember the apostle Paul's enjoinment to *"Rejoice in the Lord, alway"*? He writes much the same thing in I Thessalonians 5:16-18, saying, *"Rejoice evermore. Pray without ceasing. In every thing give thanks: for this is the will of God in Christ Jesus concerning you."* This verse tells us at least three things about praising the Lord. First, praising God should be our constant condition. Second, praise goes together with prayer. Philippians 4:6 also instructs us to let our requests be made known unto God *with thanksgiving*. Third, praise is God's will for us.

God wants us to practice praising Him because He knows it will keep our joy alive. According to Proverbs 17:22, *"A merry heart doeth good like a medicine: but a broken spirit drieth the bones."* A merry heart is a rejoicing heart. A heart that habitually rejoices in God will be healed. A heart that rejoices in the Lord will always find another reason to be joyful. Praising God is not just a discipline that gives God glory. Praising God is *good for us*. That is why God commands it—because it gives Him glory and does our hearts good.

Praising God does not mean we never allow ourselves to feel sadness or loss. We still live in a broken world. As Christians, we can simultaneously feel sorrow over what is wrong in this world while also feeling grateful for who God is and what He is doing in the world. As the apostle Paul says in I Thessalonians 4:13, we do not sorrow as those who have no hope. Praising God in everything does not mean we praise God *for* everything. We do not praise Him for pain or for evil because God is not the author of those things. However, we can praise Him even *in* our pain because we have hope that He is working all things together for our good (Romans 8:28).

Praising God—which includes rejoicing in Him, reveling in His goodness, and giving gratitude for His gifts—should be a daily ritual. In chapter 5, we mentioned keeping a happiness jar as a way to count our blessings. Perhaps your ritual of praising God should include journaling what you love about God or writing out prayers of thanksgiving to Him. Your ritual may include singing songs of praise or copying verses of thanksgiving and posting them around the house. Maybe it looks like talking to a friend about what He has been doing in your life. While the methods of praising the Lord abound, the result of praising the Lord promotes and improves the growth of joy in our lives.

Presence

Finally, we can cultivate joy through being in God's presence. We know that God is always and everywhere present. It is not a question of whether God is with us but of whether we are with God. While God is always with us, we are not always aware of His presence with us. We must consciously choose to enter His presence, to turn our minds to Him, and to allow our thoughts, attitudes, and actions to be transformed by Him. The psalmist in Psalm 16:8-9 said, *"I have set the LORD always before me: because he is at my right hand, I shall not be moved. Therefore my heart is glad, and my glory rejoiceth: my flesh also shall rest in hope."* The psalmist's joy was the result of a choice. He chose to make the Lord the center of his attention and object of his focus.

When we cannot see God in our lives, it is often because we haven't been looking for Him. We have been going about our lives, and then when things get bad, we cry out, "God, where are you?" as if He has wandered out of our lives. As the psalmist realized, benefitting from God's presence is a matter of focus. We must choose to seek God in our lives, and if we do, we will find Him. As God said through the prophet Jeremiah, *"And ye shall seek me, and find me, when ye shall search for me with all your heart"* (Jeremiah 29:13). We don't have to wait for God to come to us; God is waiting for us to come to Him.

We all have busy lives. We all live in a noisy world. So, we must do what is necessary to become aware of God's literal presence with us. Perhaps write verses, attributes of God, or Christian truths that remind you of Him on index cards and post them around the house or workplace. Just like you may have photos of your friends or family around which make you pause, think about them, and smile, you can have reminders of God that do the same. Perhaps set an alarm on your phone to go off periodically throughout the day. When the alarm rings, turn it off and clear some time and space to just be with God. Maybe that looks like talking to Him in prayer or reading His Word or meditating on a Scripture passage or truth about God. As the conclusion of Psalm 16 goes: *"Thou wilt shew me the path of life: in thy presence is fullness of joy; at thy right hand there are pleasures for evermore."*

All the ways to cultivate joy that we've discussed in this chapter could really be summarized in one word—presence. God's presence is where our joy is found and kept. Being in God's presence through daily praying to Him, pursuing purity, and practicing praise is the key to cultivating joy in our lives. Which element are you missing today? If we consistently keep these disciplines in our lives, we will discover that condition of happiness, state of contentment, and calm delight called joy.

Part 4:

Discussing Hard Issues with Hope

Chapter Nine

Addressing Suicide and the Christian

According to the Centers for Disease Control and Prevention, in 2019, suicide was the tenth leading cause of death in the United States. Among young people ages 10-34, it was the second leading cause of death. The CDC also reports that suicide was twice as prevalent as homicide in the United States in that year.[1]

Sadly, this problem is not unique to unbelievers. Christians have died by suicide as well. A biblical example would be King Saul (I Samuel 31:4). While it may be debated whether King Saul was a Christian or not, he was certainly a believer in Jehovah God. There are plenty more examples of believers in the Bible who contemplated suicide. In a season of pursuing pleasure and self-gratification, Solomon wrote in Ecclesiastes 2:17, *"Therefore I hated life; because the work that is wrought under the sun is grievous unto me: for all is vanity and vexation of spirit."* Being a Christian contemplating suicide can be uniquely lonely. Often Christians contemplating suicide do not tell anyone because

1 "Suicide," National Institute of Mental Health, accessed August 2022, https://www.nimh.nih.gov/health/statistics/suicide

they do not want to appear weak or sinful to other Christians. We could list several stories of high-profile Christians who have died by their own hand, shocking the world.

Stories like these can leave us crushed and confused. Some Christians have asked questions like, "Are Christians who commit suicide going to heaven? Would a true Christian who has the Holy Spirit within him commit suicide (something he cannot repent from)?" Those who are considering suicide themselves may ask, "If such a good Christian like that could take his own life, what reason do I have not to take mine?" Whether you have contemplated suicide or know someone who has, in this discussion, we all need these five reminders.

Remember what salvation is.

Some assume that a person who has committed or even contemplated suicide must not be a real Christian. Rather than addressing the root of his depression, they question his salvation. Perhaps the person contemplating suicide doubts his own salvation because of this struggle. Determining someone's status is not left to subjective feelings or assumptions. We must look at what the Bible teaches about salvation. I John 5:9-13 says:

> *If we receive the witness of men, the witness of God is greater: for this is the witness of God which he hath testified of his Son. He that believeth on the Son of God hath the witness in himself: he that believeth not God hath made him a liar; because he believeth not the record that God gave of his Son. And this is the record, that God hath given to us eternal life, and this life is in his Son. He that hath the Son hath life; and he*

> *that hath not the Son of God hath not life. These things have I written unto you that believe on the name of the Son of God; that ye may know that ye have eternal life, and that ye may believe on the name of the Son of God.*

This passage is written to believers— *"I have written unto you that* ***believe*** *on the name of the Son of God."* It is written so that they may have assurance of their salvation—*"that ye may* ***know*** *that you have eternal life."* This assurance is based on nothing other than God's settled word on the matter. As this passage states, if the contest is between what a person says or what God's Word says, it is best to depend on God's Word. People may question someone's salvation based on that person's deep struggles, but the Bible is the record by which we can know whether we are saved. And what does the record say? God's Word says, *"He that hath the Son hath life."* John 3:36 says, *"He that believeth on the Son hath everlasting life."* Jesus himself said, *"Verily, verily, I say unto you, He that believeth on me hath everlasting life"* (John 6:47). Believing on Jesus means trusting or depending on Him exclusively to forgive our sin and become our righteousness. The Bible says that if you have believed on Jesus for forgiveness and righteousness, then you are saved. Case closed.

Remember the truth of eternal security.

Some people have wondered whether a Christian who dies by suicide has forfeited his ticket to heaven. This idea finds no credence anywhere in the Bible. Once we have accepted Christ, our souls are safe with Jesus. Nothing can change that—not even depression or suicide. Even if we feel we are losing our grip on Him and our faith in Him, eternal security is not a matter of our holding onto Jesus. Eternal security is a matter of Jesus holding on to us. Jesus said in John 10:28-29, *"And I give unto them [my sheep or believers] eternal life; and they shall never perish, neither shall any man pluck them out of my hand. My Father, which gave them me is greater than all; and no man is able to pluck them out of my Father's hand."* Our salvation is a done deal, sealed by the Holy Spirit (Ephesians 4:30). We are triply held by the triune God! The Son holds us in the palm of His hand, the Father closes His hand over us as well, and the Spirit seals us forever.

Eternal life is not a reward for good behavior; it is a promise from God to believers. I John 2:25 says, *"And this is the promise that he hath promised us, even eternal life."* Since you did not receive eternal life because of anything you did, you cannot lose eternal life because of anything you do. As the apostle Paul was inspired to write in Romans 8:38-39, *"For I am persuaded, that neither death, nor life, nor angels, nor principalities, nor powers, nor things present, nor things to come, nor height, nor depth, nor any other creature, shall be able to separate us from the love of God, which is in Christ Jesus our Lord."* It is Christ Jesus our Lord—not ourselves—who keeps our souls secure. If even death cannot separate us from God's love in Christ Jesus, then there is nothing left that can. The love of God is greater than anything we could do.

Remember the paradox of the Christian life.

We are redeemed but still wrestling with sin. Paul said in Romans 7:19, *"For the good that I would I do not: but the evil which I would not, that I do."* After lamenting this internal struggle between his own carnality and his new desire and ability to do right, Paul finally recognizes the answer to his struggle. In verses 24-25 he says, *"O wretched man that I am! Who shall deliver me from the body of this death? I thank God through Jesus Christ our Lord."* The struggle was real for Paul, but the answer was the same as it had been before he was saved: Jesus. Just because we are saved and eternally secure does not mean that we cannot struggle deeply with darkness in this life. No struggle is beyond you, but no struggle is beyond God's grace either, as Romans 7 and 8 prove.

With this in mind, we need to face the harsh fourth reminder . . .

Suicide is sin.

It is sin because it grieves God, and it hurts others. Your body is the temple of the Holy Spirit. When you hurt your body, you grieve the Spirit.

One reason suicide grieves the Holy Spirit is that it steals glory from God. The very purpose for which we were created is to glorify God (Matthew 5:13-16). When we destroy God's creation, we dash our opportunities to glorify God in this life. We must remember that we are alive for God, not for ourselves.

An example of someone who contemplated death, but ultimately realized that he was there for God's glory is Job. In his suffering, Job concluded that death was better than life, saying in Job 7:15, "*My soul chooseth strangling, and death rather than life. I loathe it; I would not live alway: let me alone; for my days are vanity.*" When death looks more appealing than life, again we must remember why we were put on this earth. As Matthew Henry's commentary on Job goes: "Though a good man would not wish to live always in this world . . . yet he will be content to live as long as God pleases, not to choose death rather than life, because life is our opportunity of glorifying God and getting ready for heaven."[2] Job's story is a testimony to this truth! We know that Job did not stay in the depths of depression, contemplating death. In Job 13:15-16, Job famously declares, *"Though he slay me, yet will I trust in him: but I will maintain mine own ways before him. He also shall be my salvation."* Job realized that he did not have any right to his own life. It belonged to God. It was God's life to sustain, God's life to take, and God's life to save! Taking one's own life is a sin because that is essentially stealing from God. It robs God of the glory your life could bring Him.

Another reason that suicide grieves the Holy Spirit is that it seeks to take control from God. Again, since God is the Creator of life, God alone has the right to take life. Suicide is often a decision rooted in a desire to control some aspect of our lives. Since we cannot seem to control our circumstances, we seek to control how long we will be subjected to them. The thinking is that if we cannot take it any longer, we can simply bail out. At least, we have control over that. And yet God did not intend for us to have control over such things! Psalm 68:20 says, *"And unto GOD the Lord belong the issues from death."* God is the one who gets to control issues of life and death.

In Psalm 31:15, the psalmist wasn't trying to die by his own hand, but he feared dying at the hands of others. He wanted to take control, but he yielded that control to its rightful owner. In that moment, he told God, *"My times are in thy hand."* The reason that God condemns such sins as murder and, by extension, suicide is that God alone has the right to control the matters of life and death. Such a decision is not our call to make! As the modern hymn goes, "From life's first cry to final breath, Jesus commands my destiny." Suicide is the result of failure to trust in the captain of our destiny, Jesus Christ.

2 Matthew Henry. "Commentary on Job 7 by Matthew Henry," Blue Letter Bible, last modified March 1, 1996, https://www.blueletterbible.org/Comm/mhc/Job/Job_007.cfmBlue Letter Bible.

Not only does suicide grieve the Holy Spirit, but it also hurts other people. As a believer, you are a member of the body of Christ, called the Church. When a member is lost, the entire body suffers. I Corinthians 12:12-27 illustrates this by comparing the Church to a physical body with appendages or members. If someone loses an eye, he suffers a loss. The body still functions but not as well as it did before the loss. The same is true of the Church—the body of Christ. When one member is lost, especially through suicide, the entire body suffers that loss. God created us all differently so that we would fit together like puzzle pieces creating a picture of Jesus Christ. If one of those puzzle pieces is missing, the puzzle is incomplete. In other words, *you belong* in the Church. You have an important place in the body of Christ. Your unique shape and size make you an essential piece in the puzzle that creates a picture of Christ to the world around you.

When we realize that we are intimately connected to other believers and even unbelievers (because we help represent Christ to them), this reveals what a selfish decision suicide is. The people you would leave behind after suicide would be irreparably hurt by your decision. You would be in the arms of Jesus, but they would be saddled with the confusion, the grief, and the trauma of your choice. How selfish to think only of ending your own problem without thinking of the problem you force others to live with!

Often, someone assumes suicide is not a selfish decision because he tells himself that others would be better off without him. However, that's not the *real* reason for the decision. Suicide happens because he doesn't want to feel hated or resented by those people who would be better off without him. It is still about *himself*. It is still a result of *self-focus*. Suicide is the follow-through of believing the lie that your life is worthless and without hope. And this brings us to our last point.

Remember that there is always hope with God.

Because Christ is living, we are living. Christ's resurrection proves that we were created for *life*, not death. God created Adam and Eve to *live* with Him eternally. Their sin messed up that plan, but not permanently. You see, before the foundation of the world, God had planned for His Son to be the atonement for our sin. He made a way for God and man to be reconciled, for man to be restored to eternal life with Him! I Peter 1:3-5 says,

> *Blessed be the God and Father of our Lord Jesus Christ, which according to his abundant mercy hath begotten us again unto a lively hope by the resurrection of Jesus Christ from the dead, to an inheritance incorruptible, and undefiled, and that fadeth not away, reserved in heaven for you, who are kept by the power of God through faith unto salvation ready to be revealed in the last time.*

Our hope is lively because it is in a living Person—Jesus Christ. At salvation, we were recreated for eternal life! As long as He gives us breath on this earth, Jesus has a purpose for us on this earth. And when all is said and done, we have an inheritance waiting in heaven for us. Meanwhile, we are kept by God's power. If you are a Christian, you are held by the very source of hope itself! Don't give up. If there is a God in heaven and at the foot of your bed, there is hope.

If you or someone you know is contemplating suicide, remind them of these five truths. Suicide is never the answer. Rather than solve the problem, it will only create a new one. However, there is a solution to the problem of depression. While it may not be a quick fix, it is simple. With God's grace, we can make the selfless, courageous choice to face depression, rather than run away from it. And in Christ, who has already defeated sin and death, we can defeat depression. Depression must not have the last word on your life. Let Jesus have the last word on your life. He always writes good endings.

Chapter Ten

Being a Shepherd to Sufferers

We don't want to be like Job's three friends. They meant well with their pious words, but they did not edify or encourage Job. Sadly, Christians suffering from depression are often met with pious words from well-meaning friends who just don't know what to say.

According to a study from Health Services Research, "One-quarter of those who ever sought treatment for mental disorders did so from a clergy member."[3] The study shows that, although there has been a decline since the 1950s, church is still the first place many people with mental disorders go for help. If anyone should be ready to help those suffering with depression, it should be the Church. As we have seen earlier in this book, the Bible has answers, and the Church should be ready to share them with sufferers of depression.

A shepherd is someone who tends, feeds, or guards others in his care. The Lord Jesus is the ultimate example—the Good Shepherd who cares for His flock with compassion and capability. How can you, whether you are a pastor, spiritual leader, or a Christian friend be ready to shepherd sufferers of depression? Let's look at six ways you can help.

---

3 Philip S. Wang, et al., "Patterns and correlates of contacting clergy for mental disorders in the United States," *Health Services Research*, Vol. 38, No. 2 (2003): 647-73, https://www.ncbi.nlm.nih.gov/pmc/articles/PMC1360908/

Don't deny the realness of someone's depression.

Perhaps you do not see any reasons why the person should be depressed. Maybe you've never experienced depression or known anyone else who has. This does not mean that the thoughts and feelings your friend may be describing to you are not a real problem for him! Avoid responses like, "It's all in your head," or "You just need to snap out of this." While walking through the process with a depressed person can be frustrating, responses like this can only make him feel more hopeless. Instead of getting frustrated or denying the realness of the problem, listen to your friend. The best first step is to be understanding, even if you do not fully understand, by listening to what he has to say. Listen and accept that these thoughts and feelings are a legitimate problem for him. Listening, understanding, and patience are invaluable qualities of a shepherd.

Avoid making assumptions.

Whatever your experience with depression may be, you may be tempted to assume the reasons for someone else's depression. You may assume your friend is depressed because of circumstances, when really there is a harbored sin that triggered it. Perhaps you assume that your friend must be in sin, when there is a physical component to his depression. Rather than beginning the conversation with an assumption, ask your friend questions about the physical, emotional, and spiritual contributors to his own struggle. In letting your friend talk, you may discover another root problem.

Avoid toxic positivity.

Toxic positivity is trite, glib clichés we use when we don't know what else to say. The best policy is, when you don't know what to say, don't say anything; just listen! When we desperately use a cliché phrase to ease the pain, it seems like we are dismissing or trivializing our friend's suffering. Some examples of "toxic positivity" might include:

> "This too shall pass."
> "You'll get over it eventually."
> "It could be worse."
> "There is no reason to be sad."
> "But you have it so good compared to some people!"
> "Just choose to be happy."

Rather than blithe remarks, give your friend substantial hope that both acknowledges the problem and offers a solution. For example:

> "I know things are difficult right now, but it doesn't have to last forever. You don't have to accept it as your new reality."
> "This is hard, but it is not impossible to overcome."
> "This is difficult. Others have walked through this difficulty too and come out on the other side."
> "I can understand why you would feel that way, but it is possible to feel better."
> "Sometimes we struggle for unknown reasons, but we can still get through it."
> "It's not an over-night switch, but you can feel good again."

Visit your friend.

Presence matters. Just as you would visit a church member or friend sick in the hospital, visit a friend who is struggling with depression. While those with depression may not be visibly hurting, they are in just as much need of your presence as someone recovering from illness or surgery. Your physical presence can remind your friend that he is not alone, that he is loved and needed, and that his choices affect others. Perhaps set up a regular meeting with him every week or once a month. This gives you more opportunities to keep your friend accountable and encourage him.

Be patient.

You may think your friend is over it, only to find him in the same hole next week. Here you are, listening to the same struggles and going through the same conversations again. People living with depression will take steps forward and then steps backward and then more steps forward. It can be a process. They may seem receptive at first and then seem unreceptive to your help. Don't let that shake you from your plan to help them, counsel them, and walk alongside them. Consistent love, compassion, and truth is what a shepherd offers, and this will bring them through depression to the other side.

Remind your friend that no experience is wasted with God.

You and your friend may never understand what caused the depression or why this is happening, but here are some things you can both know.

First, you can know that God is able to deliver. In II Corinthians 1:8, the apostle Paul writes, *"For we would not, brethren, have you ignorant of our trouble which came to us in Asia, that we were pressed out of measure, above strength, insomuch that we despaired even of life."* Paul admits in this letter that the problems they faced *in the ministry of Christ* were so beyond measure and above their strength that they despaired of life! But the passage does not end there. Paul continues in verse 9, *"But we had the sentence of death in ourselves, that we should not trust in ourselves, but in God which raiseth the dead: who delivered us from so great a death, and doth deliever: in whom we trust that he will yet deliver us."* Paul recognized the answer to even the most intense struggles to be God Himself.

If God could deliver us from so great a death as sin and eternal separation from God, if He can deliver on the promise of the resurrection, then there is nothing from which He cannot deliver us. Paul found comfort in the truth that God had delivered and would deliver him out of all his distresses. The psalmist recognized the same truth in Psalm 34:17, saying, *"The righteous cry, and the LORD heareth, and delivereth them out of all their troubles."* The promise is not that there will be no trouble or crying but that when there is, God will hear and deliver.

You also can know that God uses sufferers to comfort other sufferers. Not only did Paul recognize the answer to his struggle to be God, but he also found comfort in the community and prayers of God's people. Paul says in II Corinthians 1:11, *"Ye also helping together by prayer for us, that for the gift bestowed upon us by the means of many persons thanks may be given by many on our behalf."* The prayers and support of a Christian community comforted Paul greatly in his ministry. This is the reason that he begins this passage by saying, *"Grace be to you and peace from God our Father, and from the Lord Jesus Christ. Blessed be God, even the Father of our Lord Jesus Christ, the Father of mercies, and the God of all comfort; Who comforteth us in all our tribulation, that we may be able to comfort them which are in any trouble"* (II Corinthians 1:2-3).

Sometimes we may wonder why we have had to struggle with depression. *How did it start? Why doesn't it go away quickly?* We will do ourselves no good dwelling on those questions. Perhaps the reason that God has allowed you to experience depression is so that He can use you in someone else's life as He used these believers in Paul's life. God wants to comfort you, but He also wants to comfort *through* you. That is enough reason to persevere.

Conclusion: Remember Our Redeemer God

As Christians, we know that God redeems suffering for our good and His glory. Someone battling depression may think, "How is my struggle with depression—a struggle with my faith, a struggle to believe that a good God even exists, a struggle to see my purpose on earth—how is that bringing Him glory?" If nothing else, the sufferer can bring Him glory by refusing to give up, by overcoming through God's grace, and by helping others who are struggling too.

This truth of redemption is evident in Psalm 30—a song David wrote for the dedication of the temple. In his life, David experienced suffering. He suffered betrayal, hatred, anxiety, loss of loved ones, and the consequences of his own sins. Yet David stood before the congregation with a song of personal redemption. David shared his personal testimony of how God had *"lifted me up... healed me... brought up my soul from the grave...kept me alive... made my mountain to stand strong... turned for me my mourning into dancing: thou hast put off my sackcloth and girded me with gladness."* With his song, David also encouraged others that *"weeping may endure for a night, but joy cometh in the morning."* In the end, David's song recognized that God had done all this for a specific purpose: *"To the end that my glory may sing praise to thee, and not be silent.* ***O*** *LORD my God, I will give thanks unto thee for ever."* The word "glory" in this psalm is poetic language for the soul or the whole being of a person. David's whole being sang God's praise. So did those who heard his song. And so should we.

God is a Redeemer. That is why He turns sorrow into gladness and suffering into glory. God knows that we are most fulfilled when pursuing our purpose of glorifying Him. How good is God that He would use even our sorrows to work out that purpose in our lives! Allow the Lord to turn your mourning into gladness. Let Him use your struggle for His glory. Make your battle plan, use your battle plan every day, and share it with others who may be like you. Perhaps, He has allowed you to go through this so you could help others see that there is a way to ditch depression and discover joy. Embrace the story God has given you! Like David, may you give thanks to your Redeemer who has *lifted* you.

Mental Battle Plan Chart

My Thought	*God's Thought*	*Scripture Support*

My Thought	God's Thought	Scripture Support